Advance Praise for *Full Body Presence*

"*Full Body Presence* is a must-read for all healthcare professionals and anyone who wants to stay healthy and continue their journey of wellness. Read Suzanne Scurlock-Durana's book many times — it's full of stories, simple-to-follow exercises, and important principles. Suzanne carefully teaches these principles to manifest change in your life. She weaves wonderful life energy throughout the tapestry of her work. Brava!"

— Ilana Rubenfeld, author of *The Listening Hand* and creator/founder of the Rubenfeld Synergy Method

D0017241

Full Body Presence

Full Body Presence

Learning to Listen to Your Body's Wisdom

Suzanne Scurlock-Durana

Foreword by John Upledger, DO, OMM

Nataraj Publishing

a division of

New World Library
Novato, California

Nataraj Publishing

a division of

New World Library
14 Pamaron Way
Novato, California 94949

Text design by Tona Pearce Myers
Illustrations by David Andor (www.wavesourcedesign.com) based on original designs by Kay Hansen

Library of Congress Cataloging-in-Publication Data
Scurlock-Durana, Suzanne.
Full body presence : learning to listen to your body's wisdom / Suzanne
Scurlock-Durana ; foreword by John Upledger.
    p.   cm.
Includes index.
ISBN 978-1-57731-860-6 (pbk. : alk. paper)
1. Craniosacral therapy. 2. Psychophysiology. I. Title.
RZ399.C73S38 2010
615.8'2—dc22   2009049583

First printing, March 2010
ISBN 978-1-57731-860-6
Printed in Canada on 100% postconsumer-waste recycled paper

g New World Library is a proud member of the Green Press Initiative.

10 9 8 7 6 5 4 3 2 1

May you arouse your
Wholehearted listening body and
Receive the news of the universe
That is singing all around us.

May we join with those throughout this world,
Visible and invisible, who tend — with heart —
The indigenous soul and beauty of this world.

— FROM "BLESSING" BY SUSAN HARPER

Contents

Foreword

I have known Suzanne Scurlock-Durana since 1983, when she took one of my first CranioSacral therapy classes and then told me she wanted to teach for me. In the twenty-five years since then, I have had the pleasure of working with her and experiencing her nurturing support and openhearted approach to life. Though Suzanne is one of our original instructors at the Upledger Institute, her passion has clearly evolved into the work she shares here in *Full Body Presence*.

This book carries an important message to those of us in health care as well as others who are in a caregiving role. The instructors, clinicians, and parents and families of the patients here at the Upledger Clinic — all benefit from learning how to stay energetically grounded and full, while holding healthy boundaries, which allows them to connect deeply without burning out.

Suzanne brings this knowledge to all of us. Her curiosity and willingness to be open to discovery have led her around the globe and back again to teach what she has learned. This instruction manual shows us how to stay calm and centered under all kinds of life stressors. She has gathered skills from the many disciplines she has studied and distilled them in a methodology that is simple, straightforward, effective, and practical.

With this book, Suzanne's work can reach a wider population. It can support what we do every day with our CranioSacral therapy patients, helping them connect more fully to themselves. The book can also help individuals address the challenges they might face when they leave our offices and return to their lives. They can maintain healthy boundaries, stay grounded, speak their truth, and replenish themselves when life takes it out of them.

Anyone can discover the process of befriending the body right here in this book. It shows you how to be friends with your body — how to relate to it as an ally rather than something to control, judge, manipulate, or push away. In short, you too can learn to achieve your own Full Body Presence.

So, as Suzanne would say, enjoy!

John Upledger, DO, OMM

Full Body Presence Terminology

To begin this guide for living with Full Body Presence, certain terms need to be defined, because we are giving language to states of conscious awareness and presence not previously discussed in this way. Memorizing these terms and definitions is not required, though, since you will learn much more about each of them throughout this book. Please read the definitions now, and then refer back to this section as needed.

FULL BODY PRESENCE: The ability to feel all parts of your body with a good flow of healthy energy moving through you. It also includes a connection to your inner and outer resources for health and a good sense of personal boundaries. Full Body Presence is the foundation of a strong, therapeutic presence.

DISRUPTED BODY PRESENCE: Impaired ability to sense or feel certain parts of your body due to physical or emotional trauma, disease, exhaustion, stress, sensory disorganization, or cultural or religious rules about body awareness. Most people have some degree of Disrupted Body Presence in any given moment due to life's demands, as well as from any of the additional factors just noted.

GROUNDING: The skill of being able to connect through your feeling senses — in a visceral way — to the earth under you or any other healthy energy resource. Full Body Presence focuses on grounding into or connecting with unconditional healthy resources.

HEALTHY RESOURCES: Resources that are life-enhancing and replenishing, such as rejuvenating connections with nature, a reassuring or empowering memory, nutritious foods, nurturing touch, a loving relationship, or a satisfying creative endeavor.

UNHEALTHY CONNECTIONS: Connections that are draining or life-taking. Unhealthy connections might involve addictive substances, such as drugs and cigarettes, or habits such as excessive alcohol consumption, overeating, compulsive gambling, or mindless shopping. Unhealthy connections also include relationships with people who are unreliable or conditional, such as controlling parents who berate you if you don't take their advice, co-workers who take advantage of you rather than support you, or lovers who betray or abuse you.

HEALTHY BOUNDARY: Your skin generally defines your physical boundary, which is not to be crossed by anyone without your permission. This boundary is the awareness of where you stop and the rest of the world begins. A healthy boundary allows nurturing resources in and filters out what is life-taking or draining. It gives you the power to say "yes" or "no" to those who want to cross your boundaries. A healthy emotional boundary does not accept words or energy directed your way that are not appropriate or healing.

CONTAINER: A metaphor for your body that gives you a sense of personal boundaries. Your energy field and all that your body is composed of naturally reside in your container.

INTERNAL LANDSCAPE: Your inner world, including sensations, images, emotions, messages, and subtle cues that inform and develop your body's innate intelligence.

NAVIGATIONAL SYSTEM: A metaphor for your body's natural capacity to discern and track what is happening internally and externally. From the information received through the navigational system of your body, you can make more aware, informed, intelligent decisions. It allows you to take action in your life, to navigate from inside yourself.

ENERGETIC AWARENESS: The ability to recognize and interpret sensory information and subtle cues in your body and environment. Your energetic awareness is an integral part of your internal landscape and navigational system.

THERAPEUTIC PRESENCE: The capacity to hold a healing space for another with your calm and centered state of being. This presence amplifies the effectiveness of whatever technical skills you already have and contributes to healthy treatment outcomes. It is a quality of being, a rapport, which feels healing, steady, and safe.

Introduction

When I was a child, I was fascinated by the invisible energy dynamics that connect us all. Growing up as a preacher's daughter on the front pew of a Baptist church, I was constantly immersed in a warm river of resonant vibration, from the rich gospel singing to the powerful, benevolent presence of my father.

I remember one night at age ten, after a particularly vibrant singing service, I was standing alone outside church in the warm, lush darkness of a Washington DC summer. Even though the service was over and the night was quiet, my insides were still buzzing. Suddenly, arising from inside my body, I felt a deep surge of connection with all of the nature around me — the tall oaks, the solid earth, the night sky. The stars seemed very close to me. I felt huge and tiny at the same time. Tears of unexplainable joy welled up from deep within my belly. With this feeling of oneness came a sense of belonging and presence. I felt full and at peace with the world. My only thought was *This is the way I was meant to be.*

For the next few days, this sense of fullness and belonging lingered in my body. I noticed that the world felt friendlier. It was easier to be a kind big sister. It was easier to live by the Sunday-school dictate to "love thy neighbor." That was my first conscious taste of directly experiencing the deep flow of life energy we all have available to us — a connection that brings us into the moment and naturally feeds our sense of Full Body Presence, making true compassion possible.

Almost everyone has experienced sacred moments or encounters of this kind. The sense of being fully present comes in all kinds of ways — perhaps a deep connectedness when holding a newborn, feeling the wind on your face while looking out over a breathtaking mountain vista, being held safely in the arms of your beloved, or experiencing the grace of meditation or prayer.

Within a few weeks of my experience, that feeling of oneness and Full Body Presence dissipated and became a distant memory. To one degree or another, this diminishment of Full Body Presence inevitably happens to us all, depending on the circumstances. Some of us barely have a chance to experience what it is like to be free, to inhabit our bodies, to have a sense of oneness, to trust ourselves and feel comfortable in the world. We easily get caught up in the cultural trance, in others' expectations, in busyness, in fear, anger, or doubt.

That summer night experience when I was ten, as well as similar experiences that followed, led me to become deeply interested in the process of becoming more fully present in each moment of my life. I studied yoga, tai chi, qigong, meditation, and Native American spiritual practices.

For the last twenty-five years, I have been bringing my knowledge to others, helping them access their own internal aliveness, using Cranio-Sacral therapy and other bodywork modalities. I have learned that when we have the skills to drop directly into the sensations within our bodies — letting the mind become our ally by simply noticing what is going on inside ourselves without judgment — the path to present moment awareness opens before us.

To clarify and facilitate this opening to present moment awareness, I distilled a set of core principles from all my studies and practices, which I refer to as the Five Principles of Full Body Presence. They help us to discern what we need most to heal and grow. They are important indicators in our internal navigational system, telling us when we are present or not. When our presence is disrupted in some way, we can then choose to move in a more life-giving direction.

My mission with this book is to help you access your connection to your body and life energy so that you can enjoy each moment more fully. This is your birthright; it serves your personal growth, creativity, and well-being. It also enables you in turn to support others and the greater good of the community. Whenever people find their inner gifts and use them, everyone benefits.

Many of the key elements of Full Body Presence have grown out of my teaching the hands-on healing system of CranioSacral therapy to healthcare professionals. This system requires its practitioners to learn to listen acutely with all their senses and to develop an ability to tune in to the subtle physical and energetic cues of the person on their therapy table.

A number of my students come to me with years of clinical experience. Although many have mastered the manual and intuitive skills needed to work with clients effectively, few know how to hold a strong, healing presence for another person. But they are hungry to know how to develop this therapeutic presence — to remain grounded in the face of the strong emotions that clients may experience in the healing process. They want to know how to be deeply empathetic without taking on a client's pain, grief, or rage, and to do so without being themselves triggered emotionally. These practitioners are also sensitive to facilitating a healing process that does not violate the client's boundaries or their own.

Often these healthcare practitioners and caregivers possess this knowledge *intuitively*, but they don't always recognize *consciously* what they are doing and so cannot apply the same energetic awareness and principles in other areas of their lives. Those principles and trained awareness are taught in this book and accompanying audio. These skills will provide you with the capacity to hold a strong therapeutic presence without burning out. In fact, in using these tools, you will probably find you have more energy for all areas of your life.

Full Body Presence is an abridged version of what I have been teaching and developing for more than twenty years in the Healing from the Core training series — tailored here for individual, self-directed use. A central part of Full Body Presence is the audio version of the Explorations. The Explorations differ from other self-help book "guided imagery techniques" exercises and meditations in that they invite you to explore, nourish, and strengthen *your unique* internal landscape by developing an increasing awareness of your body. These are not affirmations or prescriptions. The Explorations are an energetic awareness–building practice, which integrates body, mind, and spirit, and connects you to your deep inner knowing. You will find yourself reclaiming your innate energy, resilience, and guidance.

This book is meant to be read straight through, without jumping around. If you find the content in a chapter familiar, skim it — but please read sequentially, because the skills taught here build on each other. Every chapter and each Exploration has a distinct purpose. The Explorations also build on each other, so please initially listen to the audio in order as well. The audio portion of this book is central to this material. Simply reading the transcripts in the back of the book will not convey the information fully. Have the audio ready to play now, so you can listen to it easily when the time comes.

These instructions are based on my many years of experience. I have guided thousands of people through this process with amazing results. Enjoy!

Chapter One

Out of Touch

Our bodies are the containers for our spirits. They are incredible navigational systems that inform us constantly, from our gut instincts to our heart's deepest yearnings. But take a quick look around you, and you won't see much acknowledgment of this truth. We are taught to ignore our gut instincts and to be polite instead. We are taught to ignore physical hunger and to strive to be stick thin if we are women. We are rewarded for overworking, often at the expense of our health — raising our stress levels even more. We are taught to live in our heads and to ignore the body's wisdom.

As we lose touch with our bodies, our healthy resilience suffers. The expression "Speed kills" refers to more than highway statistics. The speed of modern technology, combined with the sheer volume of information thrown at us on any given day, is enough to make us feel as though we cannot slow down and breathe if we want to keep up. The complexity in our lives can be overwhelming.

The good news is that, although changing slowly, the present state of body awareness in the United States is beginning to improve, as seen in the increasing numbers of people going for bodywork and attending yoga or movement classes. Along with this growing recognition of the value of the mind-body connection, there is a growing awareness of the problems alienation from our body creates. Such awareness gives us that much more incentive to learn to be fully present in our bodies and our lives. This is particularly so if we hope to be able to help others in a way that is more rewarding and less stressful.

Stress in the Healthcare and the Caregiving Worlds

Teaching in the healthcare world, I see the effects of Disrupted Body Presence exhibited in the exhaustion and stress-related illnesses of my students. The effect of burnout on bodyworkers, caregivers, and other healthcare professionals is well known. This burnout in turn creates serious consequences for the individual, the family, and society.

A burned-out healthcare provider with diminished therapeutic presence can miss important cues and signals, increasing the risk that mistakes will be made. This is further aggravated by the mountains of paperwork now required with medical treatment, which leave little or no time for the nurturing parts of the job. Staff cuts leave those still employed to do the work of two people, but without the healthy resources these workers need.

More important, very few healthcare providers and caregivers are taught how to stop, tune in, and take care of themselves so that they can more effectively take care of others without burning out. In fact, the default stance for many working in health care is to give without any thought of themselves. Their satisfaction and self-worth are measured by the results of their efforts on behalf of others. Self-care is often seen as selfish or self-centered. Another risk for caregivers and healthcare providers is that they can easily absorb a patient's tension and fear, unless they know how to hold healthy boundaries.

Some healthcare modalities teach practitioners to distance themselves from a patient or a client. This can work to a degree, but it also effectively numbs a healthcare provider's ability to participate in the positive, life-giving aspects of the work. The care provided is then limited, and compassion is missing. Such an approach creates a mechanical healthcare system rather than a conduit for deep caring and healing that benefits all involved. Burnout is then not far behind. The need for restorative steps is clear.

Mind-Body-Spirit Connection

In recent years a great deal has been discovered about the intimate interplay between mind, emotions, and body. We have clear evidence of how emotions are intimately connected to physical distress and illness. Yet for all the exciting new therapeutic approaches for working directly with the body to restore health and awareness, the value of Full Body Presence is still not well recognized.

The aspect of sensory awareness in Full Body Presence — the grounded connection with our body and the world around us — can play a major role in healing physical symptoms and illnesses. It can assuage and ultimately transform fear, doubt, and alienation into a sense of trust and confidence in oneself and life as a whole. Developing sensory awareness is also a powerful means of personal transformation. The strong therapeutic presence that emerges is of vital importance for both the caregiver and the one receiving care.

Full Body Presence also leads us to a more solid connection with our innate spirit and energy. And this connection can become the ever-present background against which we live our lives — instead of the serendipitous minutes of connection and ecstasy we may otherwise experience occasionally.

In many spiritual traditions, heaven is synonymous with being fully connected to the Divine, to our spiritual source. Yet this visceral sense of connection — which is or should be a given — slips away from us as we are socialized to fit in to our hierarchical and compartmentalized culture.

Unfortunately, elements of our educational system, cultural practices, and even religious doctrines speak in terms of dominating the world and our environment and of controlling our bodily functions and thoughts — as if we were somehow separate from the rest of creation. Our emphasis on speed, instant gratification, outward appearances, staying competitive, and retaining power without regard to the long-term outcome leaves us little time for feeling and meeting our deeper physical, emotional, and spiritual needs.

In this milieu, our deeper *felt* needs are relegated to a lesser status. With regard to large or small issues, the wisdom of the body and its signals are suspect and not to be trusted in our culture. We typically give our thoughts more weight than our nonlinear inner knowing. We put our trust in outside experts to figure out what to do in our lives, rather than taking external data and going inside ourselves and connecting to our deeper wisdom to learn what is best for us. When we don't trust our internal awareness, we neglect our sensory awareness and create a sense of separation from our world, which is reinforced as we continue to ignore our inner world.

Origins of Disrupted Body Presence

Trust in our instincts and awareness can be eroded in many ways. Perhaps there was a time as a child when you felt sick but were told you were fine. This is how we begin to doubt our own internal cues. Perhaps you were grief-stricken when a friend moved away, but you were told that your grief was shameful, not important, or at the very least unreasonable (because you had plenty of other friends, right?). Again, you were being taught to mistrust your feelings, and so you began to lock away your grief whenever it arose in the future.

Or perhaps you had an uncle who gave you a creepy feeling when he hugged you at family reunions, but when you mentioned it to another adult, you were told to "Quit being silly and thinking such a thing about your uncle!" So you began to distrust your internal knowing, which told you your boundaries were being violated in some way. You may have had a friend you loved with all your heart, but others made fun of you for loving so openly and wholeheartedly. Maybe you were rejected, and you began to close down how much love you let yourself feel or the level of inspiration for living you allowed yourself to experience. In all these examples, your body was telling you something important, but those around you tried to convince you that what you were sensing wasn't real or valid.

Trauma and Defense Responses

No matter where we grew up, we have all had to adapt in order to survive and be accepted, conforming to the expectations of our families, religious traditions, and culture. Depending on our innate temperament and the level of repression to which we were subjected, we behave according to our own unique adaptations and defenses. Many of our idiosyncratic defense mechanisms may have originally served as brilliant survival tactics, particularly if we overcame traumatic events or circumstances. However, in most cases, these adaptations are now obsolete. They contribute to our sense of separation from ourselves and our world and now function as impediments to our happiness.

When traumatic events happen to us, the natural human tendencies are to respond to the stress by freezing, numbing, wanting to run, or fighting back to defend ourselves. Trauma can cause a temporary or a long-term disruption of our Full Body Presence. When our focus is on survival alone, our nervous system automatically goes into a high state of arousal, which can lead to skewed perceptions and reduced energetic awareness that can affect us in detrimental ways, especially when the traumatic event is long gone. Trauma often causes us to lose touch with our internal navigational system and the wisdom and safety it can provide. When we are not fully present in our bodies because of past or present trauma, we have a disruption in our system that needs to be resolved.

Building Your Present Moment Awareness Skills

If at times you feel overwhelmed by your feelings, you will find the audio Explorations can help you learn to develop your body and energy field as a container that can hold and modulate the whole range of human emotions. Building and continually strengthening this container enables you to have feelings and to learn from them, rather than having to constantly suppress them for fear of being overwhelmed or embarrassed by them. During times of acute stress or personal tragedy, this is particularly important.

In twenty-five years of teaching this work, I have watched thousands of students not only understand but also come to embody present moment awareness. I've watched students move into the deeper resonance and connection to life that is our birthright as human beings. It is in this state of flow and connection with our deepest spiritual knowing that we can experience the peace of being alive and fully embodied in each present moment.

LISTEN:
Your body is speaking to you.

To download the free audio tracks
for this book or order a CD
for a small fee plus shipping, visit

www.healingfromthecore.com,
click on the Full Body Presence Download link,
and enter the password *presence*

or write to us at

Healing from the Core
P.O. Box 2534
Reston, VA 20195-2534

Chapter Two

How I Learned to Trust My Body's Signals

My childhood awareness of the invisible energy dynamics con-necting us all, which I shared with you in the Introduction, slowly continued to expand after that summer night in Washington DC. When I was seventeen, I received my first big lesson in how my body could act as a barometer capable of sensing these invisible energy dynamics, in-forming me of the rightness or wrongness of a situation. Many of us have had a gut sensation when something felt really off — a sense of danger. Had I then had the confidence to trust my body's signals, which I do have today, the following story would have played out quite dif-ferently.

One Saturday night, deep in the warm summer of 1971, I was with an old friend, who unbeknownst to me was in withdrawal after a long stint of being awake on amphetamines. As we sat together, having a normal friendly teenage conversation in his car, in the parking lot outside of a neighborhood pool party, I began to feel a strange but distinct uneasiness in my gut. It was not a response to the tone of his voice or the topic of discussion. The uneasiness continued for well over half an hour, but I continued to ignore it because it seemed unreasonable to feel uncomfortable with my friend. He was such a close friend, like an older brother to me. Besides, I thought it would have been impolite to say anything about it.

The next thing I knew, his hands were around my throat, and he was strangling me. He was so strong I quickly and completely passed out. When I regained consciousness, I was trembling all over. My head was pressed against the car door. My friend was plastered to the other side of the front seat, behind the wheel, obviously shocked and horrified at what he had done. He apologized profusely. I, too, was in serious shock. Every cell in my body screamed at me to get out of the car *now*. This time I listened. I managed to open the door and crawl across the parking lot to a friend's car, where help was waiting. It took years of emotional healing and bodywork to melt the internal scars of betrayal and fear from that event. If I had paid attention to my gut and honored the message it was giving me, I could have avoided the whole situation.

Several years later, having established trust in my gut knowing, I was able to avoid another potential disaster. I was on a date with a popular basketball player in college. We were drinking and laughing at a party in someone's dorm room. The music was loud, and people were having a good time. At one point, however, I noticed that people were leaving. Soon my date and I would be the only ones left. My gut gave me that alarm signal I had experienced years earlier. This time I listened. I made up an excuse about needing to go to the bathroom, but I left for good. Later I discovered that this basketball player had date-raped several women on campus. Although I had learned the hard way initially, I did learn to listen to my gut.

What about the other body signals of this invisible world of energy dynamics? I learned more when I gained an understanding of breath and conscious movement and brought these practices into my life. Just before I left for college in the fall of 1971, I took my first yoga class. I loved it. Somehow, I instinctively knew that the conscious awareness I was being taught about breath, movement, and slowing down would bring me closer to connecting intentionally with the experiences I had previously undergone only serendipitously. As I faithfully practiced the yoga asanas and meditation each day, I began to notice a quieting in my system that I had never known before, as well as a growing ability to hear what my body was saying to me.

By my last year of college, I had firsthand experience of how my intention and Full Body Presence could combine to create a powerful synergy. I was in a dance performance in which I was a tree. My entire role was to stand solidly, center stage. Another dancer, a young man about forty pounds heavier than me, had to climb up one side of me and down the other. I was chosen for the role because I could stand most strongly and firmly. I did this by taking my conscious awareness inside my body to feel myself growing roots, like a big oak tree, down through the stage floor and into the earth. Once I was rooted, I was almost immovable. Although I could walk away whenever I wanted to, I had nonetheless created a strong connection to the ground beneath me.

Everyone was amazed when I held the weight of my fellow dancer. For me, this ability was simply an extension of what I had been playing with for several years. Later, I would learn that in the martial arts and certain meditation practices, this same use of intention and body awareness is well known. But I was discovering all this on an adventure of my own, exploring intention, energetic connection, and Full Body Presence.

My Parents' Presence

My parents' willingness to continue growing throughout their lives was a great example for me. And the ways in which they were limited by their life experiences affected me as well. For instance, my mom took me to my first yoga class, which was a pivotal part of my journey. Mom also has a gentle, quiet energy and a huge, warm heart, but like many women in her generation, when I was growing up, she couldn't model healthy boundaries. She let people walk all over her, had a hard time asking for what she needed, and put everyone else's needs first. So, while I learned to be a warmhearted presence from my mother, I was also left with huge questions about being powerful and female.

My father was an incredible thinker and a powerful public speaker. I grew up wanting to be like him. He had a presence that commanded attention, which gave me permission to do the same. The flip side was that his public presence exhausted him. What I later discovered is that my father had ready access only to his mind and upper body, which left him with a Disrupted Body Presence and explained his depletion and exhaustion at the end of every Sunday service.

My parents were unable to convey to me an appreciation for my lower body and all that the lower body represents — gut instinct, sexuality, intense creativity, movement, and grounding. Although I had a loving family, as I grew into adulthood, I understood that both my parents had deep issues of shame around their sexuality. Both experienced childhood traumas that caused them to energetically withdraw from their lower bodies and severely disrupted their Full Body Presence. They did not pass on the abuse they had received, but their fear of lower-body energy left a gaping hole in my understanding of the lower body in a healthy person.

As is often the case, my religion taught me to judge and control my body. We were Baptists. Full-hearted singing and righteous (upper-body) presence were modeled, but the energetic awareness of the lower body — *legs, feet, and pelvis* — were not understood to be vital for supporting a compassionate heart and full experience of life.

Moving Beyond My Legacy

Yoga and meditation helped me to bridge the gap left in me. I began to feel more present throughout my entire body. And while I am eternally grateful for what I learned, I also found limitations in these ancient systems. They were highly codified and rule-bound as to how one should experience the body. The underlying premise is that the breath and the body it fills are to be brought under control. I was still being told how to experience my body rather than freely exploring its natural and unique exquisiteness.

My understanding of many religious and spiritual systems is that being connected to life, to God, to the Universal All, the Tao, whatever name one uses, ultimately means controlling and leaving the body — not fully inhabiting it. This didn't feel right to me. After all, I was learning to trust my body and my gut feelings. So while I continued my daily yoga and meditation practices — growing my "energy muscles" and learning to focus — I instinctively kept searching for something more.

The birth of my first child catalyzed a journey that made my spiritual practice a more practical part of my life. My seventeen years of having an hour a day for spiritual practice was over when I had my baby. All new parents can relate to this. I could no longer take time to cultivate the steady peacefulness my hour of spiritual practice provided. I now needed a way to connect to healthy resources in the midst of my busy life instead.

The same year my daughter was born, I also began teaching Cranio-Sacral therapy regularly, so I needed to find something that would support my strong and integrated presence as a teacher in the classroom. How could I bring Full Body Presence to my life with all the challenges that parenthood and work brought? It was at this point that the Five Principles of Full Body Presence were first conceived.

I began to distill the wisdom I had learned from the various teachers and spiritual practices I had known — from the lessons learned as a child on that front pew, bathed in the resonance of church singing, all the way to lessons on hearing the whispers of wisdom from the animals, trees, and rocks, which my indigenous teachers taught me. I was clarifying the principles for setting and following a laserlike, focused intention as well as surrendering to the all-encompassing flow of life energy available to all of us. I was also learning how trusting in this flow opened more possibilities for my healing and growth and how feeling life's energy in my own body and letting it integrate throughout my system gave me more access to my gifts and vitality. I began to recognize how using my mind as an ally, instead of a critic, expanded my capabilities as a therapist, teacher, mother, and wife. Finally, learning to choose from moment to moment what was most life-giving helped me to move from the exhaustion and overwhelm of infant care and healing work to the joy of my family and life again.

I needed to be able to discern a healthy direction in my life on a moment's notice. I needed to understand how the navigational system of my body operated optimally and what to do when it was awry. I needed to have clear, simple questions to ask myself that would guide my day. The Five Principles did that for me. They are tried and true guidelines that work hand in hand with the Explorations.

In all the years that I have been peeling away layers and learning to move into the truth of who I am, I have been deeply challenged and deeply rewarded. Walking this path feeds and amplifies my creativity. I have developed confidence in what I am doing because I have learned to act from the core of who I am. And I have witnessed this same process of evolution in my students over the last twenty-five years. They consistently tell me how this work catalyzed them into making their dreams a reality, helped them make peace with things in their lives that they were struggling with, or allowed them to deal with a personal tragedy without shutting down.

As I removed the layers of fear,
doubt, resistance, anger, and denial,
my life's purpose became increasingly clear.
Now let's bring clarity to your life.

Chapter Three

The Five Principles of Full Body Presence

Like signposts on the path of life, the Five Principles of Full Body Presence can be used to help you create optimal, healthy living. They identify key concepts about the invisible energy dynamics of the universe. As you explore the deeper meanings of these principles, you may find that the framework they present is familiar. The reason is that these principles, in one form or another, underlie the core teachings of most major religions. By understanding and then using these principles in your everyday life, you are not only embracing skills that can heal your life and bring you greater joy but also gaining access to greater support for deepening your own spiritual practices, whatever they happen to be.

The illustration of the Five Principles of Full Body Presence (see page 23) honors the symbol of the circle — a geometric shape found everywhere in nature. Everything comes full circle, as with the life, death, and rebirth cycles in the seasons on our planet. We all live within the circle of Earth and its magnetic field and sea of energy. From the circular shape that we find in the structure of our cells to the stars in the heavens, we are all interconnected.

As seen in the Medicine Wheel of indigenous cultures, no one part of the circle dominates or is more important than any other element. The circle establishes balance and the understanding that everything has its place and is important in some way. In that same vein, the Five Principles are interconnected in what they teach us. If the principle of Trusting is a challenge for you, you may find that to trust more fully you need to apply the Expanding principle in order to see your world more clearly and accurately. With a more expanded lens on the world, you can then work with the principle of Choosing more healthy resources for yourself, which helps you create better outcomes. This in turn helps you with Trusting and opening to new possibilities. All the while, your Full Body Presence is increasing.

The Five Principles provide guidelines for working with the invisible sea of energy in your life at physical, emotional, mental, and spiritual levels. Each is of equal importance to your well-being. Alone or in combination, each principle will show up in your life at times of stress or healing, demanding your attention. The correct starting point or entry into your own circle of healing or transformation may shift with each new circumstance in your life.

Sometimes you may find that you are working primarily with one principle for a while — for instance, the principle of Feeling the Presence of Life Energy in Your Body. You may recognize that you have trouble feeling much of anything internally, which makes decision making difficult as you constantly second-guess. So, you begin to practice the skills taught here, and one day when a stressful situation pops up, you realize that you have learned to effectively apply the principle of Feeling. Where before you would have struggled to know what you felt or wanted, now you drop inside easily and know exactly what to do.

This mastery may then lead you to the principle of Choosing Nourishing Resources Moment to Moment, as you realize that now you can choose more wisely for yourself because your inner compass is operational. Now you can weave the fabric of your life with healthy resources, which leave you feeling more energized and steady.

Usually, what you need will call to you as you read this chapter. Recognizing which principles resonate with you and then addressing what they are pointing out to you will enable you to increase your Full Body Presence — and in turn enhance your life, health, and creative process. Let's get started.

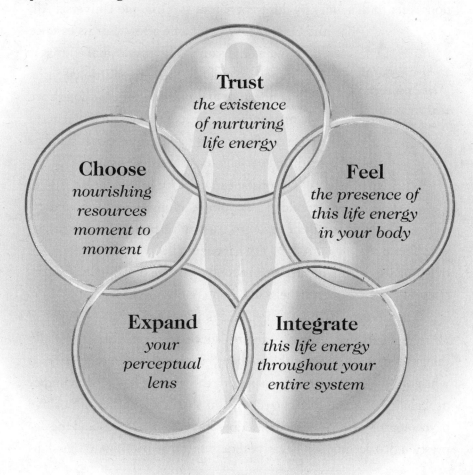

Trust
*the existence
of nurturing
life energy*

Choose
*nourishing
resources
moment to
moment*

Feel
*the presence of
this life energy
in your body*

Expand
*your
perceptual
lens*

Integrate
*this life energy
throughout your
entire system*

PRINCIPLE 1

TRUST the Existence of Nurturing Life Energy

Trusting that there is an unlimited source of nourishing,
life-giving energy in the Universe allows you to relinquish
fear, live from trust, and recognize that you are loved
and supported throughout your life.

Quantum physics has shown us that at a molecular level we are all connected, swimming together in this sea of energy. Many spiritual traditions refer to this unity by different names — God, the Universal All, the One, the Tao, to name a few. But its essence remains the same. The primordial source is timeless, endless, and unconditional in its connection and offering to us. Though we may not feel connected in certain moments to this sea of energy, we all have access. It supplies all of us with an ever-abundant healthy resource.

I trust my ability to connect to healthy resources.

This field of energy is a constant support for leading healthy, vital lives. As you develop confidence in your relationship to this boundless source of energy, it will be easier to trust and handle what life brings you. This principle of trusting is what energetically underlies the work of a broad spectrum of successful people — some of whom have written prolifically about self-help and living one's best life.

When Norman Vincent Peale says in his primer, *The Power of Positive Thinking*, "Always picture 'success,' no matter how badly things seem to be going at the moment," he is referencing the fact that when one trusts and envisions support, the support has a much higher probability of being recognized when it shows up. Father of positive psychology Martin Seligman describes how the pessimism and the depression that accompany negative thoughts can be overcome. The skills he teaches rest on reestablishing trust, because it opens the doors to possibilities previously not seen.

In *The Speed of Trust,* Stephen R. Covey's foreword examines a whole new facet to the principle of Trusting when he points out that the advantage in today's business world is in how fast a product or a service can be brought to market. He clearly delineates how trust increases the efficiency of organizations, while low trust impedes the whole process by creating hidden agendas, interpersonal conflict, defensive communications, and win-lose thinking. He says:

An attitude of trust and trustworthiness affects all aspects of my life.

> Trust is like the aquifer — the huge water pool under the earth — that feeds all of the subsurface wells. In business and in life, these wells are often called innovation, complementary teams, collaboration, empowerment... these wells themselves feed the rivers and streams of human interaction, business commerce, and deal making.

This principle speaks to what happens energetically when an attitude of trust is established and applied in our lives. When we learn to trust that support is there for us and lean into that trust, it leads to a doorway of many new possibilities. This is much more powerful than simply visualizing a positive outcome and tenaciously trying to hold on to it.

One of my colleagues tells the story of her basketball-playing, eleven-year-old son. His coach was working with the team to set up positive visions of themselves and their playing abilities. Unfortunately, her son's vision was to be a perfect player, the star of the team. Although it was an admirable goal, every time he missed a shot, it crushed him and crippled his playing. His entire vision would disintegrate. Between games, my colleague quietly suggested to her son that he choose a vision

I trust that I am supported by my world.

of himself playing his best, with his team supporting one another. He liked that vision better; it opened possibilities without absolutes. Not only did his attitude improve dramatically, so did his playing!

The capacity to be open to discovery is an important first step in any healing, growing, or manifesting process, and being open requires trust. Many people can agree with this principle in theory but still find it hard to trust in moments of uncertainty or depletion. Or they become overwhelmed when it appears that there is no support available. But it is when life gets challenging that we most need to remember to trust. We have all had painful or scary experiences at some point in our lives. Our world or certain aspects of it suddenly feel dangerous and unfriendly, or we decide we are somehow at fault.

When either of those decisions becomes a default stance in our lives, often unconsciously, we can find ourselves, particularly in times of stress or uncertainty, struggling to find healthy resources and solutions. It is important to remember that our basic underlying default stance is what cuts off our capacity to trust in a supportive source of energy we *can* tap into. Without trust, Full Body Presence is disrupted.

Many of us know people who are surrounded by love or supported in some way that they cannot experience because they are constantly on guard, waiting for the other shoe to drop. In all likelihood, they have developed strategies, which don't work very well, to tightly control their world in a misguided effort to keep it safe. Their Disrupted Body Presence prevents them from seeing the support that is available to them. They walk right by it.

In what areas of my life do I trust in myself and my abilities?

How do you know if this principle needs your attention? It does if under stress or in personally upsetting situations, you have thoughts or resort to actions or words that reflect fear or anxiety. Fear and anxiety distract us from the healthy resources and possibilities that might otherwise assist us. This difficulty can show itself in any number of ways. It might take the form of blaming others instead of taking appropriate responsibility for moving yourself in a more positive and helpful direction. On the other hand, you might be taking too much responsibility and misguidedly blaming yourself. Perhaps you withdraw, contract, or freeze so that you don't have to experience fully what you fear will happen. Maybe you attack someone close to you in a confused attempt to fend off a real or an imagined enemy.

Clearly, this principle of Trusting the Existence of Nurturing Life Energy affects decision making. Decisions based on trust differ significantly in quality and results from decisions based on fear. Trust creates an openness to discovery, which in turn unlocks the door to more of life's possibilities. It also opens us to the energy of life so that we are connected to what we need.

When you are in a state of trust, where do you feel that sense of trust in your body?

One of my colleagues reports that when she is in a tight spot and cannot actually feel trusting of this support, she acts as if she does trust or imagines herself having a conversation with someone she knows trusts. Then she diligently directs herself to take actions that open up those new possibilities. She finds that the trust and support inevitably follow.

So, the key is to train yourself to remember that this unconditional source of energy does exist and to pause and connect with it in whatever way you can in each moment. Possibilities and options will become clear and more accessible, eclipsing the cycle of negative thinking, and you will begin to trust again.

When you reach the part in this book where you are asked to listen to Exploration 3, you will be guided in a process of deep healing, rewiring your nervous system to be able to accept a new, more pleasurable, healthy reality. When practiced regularly, relaxation and receptivity to new possibilities are supported.

PRINCIPLE 2

FEEL the Presence of Life Energy in Your Body

*Feeling your internal connection to life energy
as a natural state of being opens your awareness
to discover a sense of belonging, reclaim your inner wisdom,
and experience vitality and joy.*

The ability to feel a sense of connection to the larger universal energy honors the innate intelligence of your body as an internal compass. As you deepen this connection, you learn to navigate by using your internal compass, rather than the world's expectations or input from others alone.

With Principle 1, *trust* points out that we are all connected, all the time, to the universal source that makes up the field of energy we live in. Principle 2, *feeling*, addresses the felt sense of connection to ourselves and the world around us, which is our birthright. When we allow ourselves to experience this deeply felt sense of connection, there may be a tingling, warmth, elation, openheartedness, calm, quiet, joy, knowing, flow, creative thought, powerful ease, nourishing fullness, or bliss. As Candace Pert says in *Molecules of Emotion*, "We're hardwired for bliss." We operate best from that state of connection, as conscious participants in the flow of life. We experience a visceral sense of belonging — in our own bodies! This state of feeling fully alive is our birthright.

When you have a sense of spiritual connection and oneness with life, how do you experience it in your body?

There are many ways to consciously connect with the ever-present source of life energy. You may already have ways that increase your energetic awareness, such as walking on the beach, hiking in the woods, sitting on a massive rock, feeling a wind brush your body, reveling in the warm sun on your face, or being rocked gently by ocean waves. The connection available to you in nature can also be felt in a calming breath, a prayer, a meditation, or in the resonance of singing or chanting.

In Exploration 2, the exercise uses imagery to connect with the rich field of the earth — grounding, feeling firmly rooted, receiving whatever would most nurture and nourish us in that moment. With each repetition of this Exploration, we strengthen and reaffirm our ability to feel our connection, deepening our energetic awareness and refining our ability to navigate through the world from inside our bodies.

With this innate sense of connection to life comes a natural sense of vitality and joy. I saw this most clearly in both my children when they were younger. When my son was two, I remember being amazed by his spontaneous, unimpeded flow of energy, curiosity, and aliveness. The delight and openness with which he drank in all life had to offer, and the generosity in this outpouring of love in return, were a pleasure to be around. Looking back now, I would say he had exquisitely tuned energetic awareness, which allowed him to live in his Full Body Presence.

When you are feeling most energized, where do you feel it? What do you think?

One afternoon at the circus, when the elephants burst through the curtains in all their glory and glittery costumes, I thought my son would burst with joy. His eyes lit up. He shrieked and laughed and clapped and called to them, drinking them in with all of his senses. Their smell filled the tent, the lights glittered off of them, and they strutted in all of their magnificence. He was enthralled. Full Body Presence at its best!

But when someone would reject him or life wasn't giving him what he needed, my son's grief could be all-encompassing as well. He was connected to it all, and the waves just rolled right through. Over the

Disrupted Energy Flow

Energy blockage in neck creates reduced flow to the head

Trapped energy formations/masses from old traumas or injuries

Energy flow moves around the heart but is reduced through the heart

In this figure, the energy flow through the heart and throat are disrupted by past traumas or injuries. This is a common human experience — having either large or small areas, obvious or subtle places, that don't feel as connected to the rest of us.

course of a day, he could move through a broad spectrum of feelings — pleasure and pain, ecstasy and disappointment, anger and sweet tenderness — because he lived in the present moment, in the flow of life. Watching him, I recognized the capacity for connection to life we all have, however buried or repressed it might be.

Because of life experiences over time that have caused us to stifle or shut down our own connection to the fullness of life, most of us have to relearn how to access it. We reclaim that connection through an energetic awareness of the internal landscape of our body, which reveals our inner wisdom. Like an inner compass of deep knowing, our innate cellular intelligence informs us constantly. It is a hunch that something is off in a relationship or a sense of rightness about a project that makes no sense logically yet makes our heart sing. It might be a direction we somehow know we need to take, or it might be someone we instinctively know we should avoid at all costs.

This deep wisdom emerges from all parts of us. Sometimes we will feel an ache in our heart or a tightening in our gut. At other times, we might hear it as a whisper of instruction about a confusing person or situation. Wisdom might come as a memory of an event that reminds us of something we need to learn in this moment. The body's inner compass of wisdom is always with us — though we don't always listen or immediately know what it is saying.

I recognize and honor my gut feelings and my heart's desires, and I include both in my life choices.

It's not the norm in Western culture to listen to our insides, to take the time to slow down and focus on internal awareness and to make decisions based on our deep inner knowing. Instead, we tend to be driven to move forward and accomplish everything that is expected of us, regardless of what we truly want (if we even know what that is) or how we are feeling deep within.

If anyone asks, we smile and say we're doing fine, as we run on automatic pilot. We focus on doing rather than being.

When the experience of feeling connected to yourself, your internal landscape, is disrupted, then fear, hopelessness, despair, or overwhelm often arise. You may feel isolated or have a sense of not belonging anywhere. Physically the disruption can manifest as intense pain, a dull background ache, an emptiness, a sense of clenching, or feeling run down. When this happens, it's important to acknowledge that you're feeling separate and to notice what that feels like in your body. Having that awareness of the disruption in your system enables you to make a new decision to move in the direction of establishing a connection to what nurtures you. It's also important to understand that the experience of feeling separate, though it seems very real, is only a perception. You are never actually disconnected from life.

Remember, we exist within this sea of energy all the time, whether we are conscious of it or not, whether we choose to acknowledge it or not. When you are able to feel this healthy life force within your body, you not only regain your sense of belonging but also tap a vast reservoir of intuitive knowledge and guidance toward the vitality of a healthier, more joyful life.

Another issue that comes up with this principle is looking at what can impede or support our ability to feel our insides. Nurturing physical touch encourages a healthy internal sense of self and increases our energetic awareness, while a lack of nurturing touch creates a sense of numbness or pain. My clinical experience has shown me that a huge lack of nurturing touch exists in our world today. This diminishes our ability to sense our internal landscape and to remain steady and grounded. When touch is not safe and nurturing, our automatic response is to pull away from it. Touch has been further sexualized and exploited in our culture, greatly contributing to the sense of separation currently so prevalent among us.

Lack of loving touch also affects our ability to grow, mature, and flourish as a species. We know from recent infant and child attachment research that a child who feels a secure physical and emotional connection to at least one parent develops the neural pathways for resilience. Those that miss out on nurturing physical and emotional connections have a much harder time consoling themselves, calming their anxieties, and tolerating high levels of pleasure and excitement.

I accept and enjoy healthy, nurturing touch.

Nurturing, noninvasive touch is a major component in developing the healthy resilience we all require in today's world. But many of us grew up in households operating from a touch deficit — which we may not even be aware of. We have not experienced, simply do not know, the deep nourishment that can be felt from consistent caring touch. As Ashley Montague so clearly pointed out in his landmark book, *Touching: The Human Significance of the Skin*, nurturing touch is a biological need, an imperative for the healthy development of all infants. The worldwide research he shares shows that children thrive when they are held and bonded with as much as each baby needs and wants.

Think about your history with nurturing touch. Many of us have no context with which to understand the deep nourishment I describe here. We don't have a frame of reference for something we have never experienced. If this applies to you, you may find that you don't reach for, feel comfortable with, or easily accept the healthy, sensual, and pleasurable connections of being alive that healing touch can provide. Those who were held and touched enough as infants and children have a better chance of living with an expanding capacity to experience pleasure and to reach more easily for healthy resources throughout life.

The good news is that we can heal this. By creating channels for nurturing touch in our present-day lives, we can establish the neural pathways of healthy resilience that we missed when we were younger. The latest research in brain anatomy and function shows that the neural plasticity of the brain and nervous system continues in response to new input throughout our lives. Changes in our nervous system can be brought about powerfully by current ongoing experiences.

Healing influences of touch can take many forms — a nurturing partner or friend who hugs you frequently; getting regular bodywork such as massage, CranioSacral therapy, or any other healing system that really listens to the body and responds to it with nurturing care; or a pet that snuggles and cuddles with you. It could even be something as simple as sleeping on sheets that feel wonderful to your skin or taking baths or showers that give your skin the feeling of warmth or coolness it craves. There are many ways to create for ourselves the healthy pleasures of touch, which nourish our nervous system.

Every nurturing, pleasurable sensation we can let in, everything we learn, and every healthy intimate connection we make cause millions of neurons to fire together, forming new physical interconnections within the body. These neural networks support healthy resilience, and resilience allows us to feel a reliable and consistent sense of connection to life. When our energetic awareness grows within this framework, we can navigate wisely from within our bodies. We admit new possibilities for greater vitality and joy into our lives. Our Full Body Presence becomes the foundation for our present moment awareness.

PRINCIPLE 3
INTEGRATE Life Energy Throughout Your Entire System

Integrating a felt sense of nurturing life energy throughout your entire body helps you establish a full personal container with strong, flexible, healthy boundaries.

When you consciously choose to open all your channels to receive nurturing energy, you gain access to more parts of yourself. You will also find yourself in the present moment more easily and more often. You create a strong container from which to process and heal your own pain, and you gain the capacity to hold a powerful healing presence for someone else.

You learn intimately where you stop and the rest of the world begins. This is what is meant when we talk about having healthy boundaries. It is easier to maintain healthy boundaries when you have a nourishing flow of energy throughout your body, your container. Your skin and the energy field that flows through and around it provide a boundary to be respected by others.

When your container is full of nourishing energy, you have a clearer sense of yourself. You can choose to connect more deeply with the world around you, and you are clear when you respond to negative energy — be it from a client, a family member, or a stranger.

With healthy boundaries around vital, nourishing energy, you also gain a greater capacity to hold a healing space, a strong therapeutic presence, for another person, without depleting yourself. In fact, the more you practice this principle, the more likely you are to come out of such interchanges with

I can sense when someone crosses my boundaries and say "no" when something does not feel right to me.

more energy rather than less. The Full Body Presence that is the signature of a full container enables you to hold this space for another person effortlessly. Your therapeutic presence provides a calm, centered quality of being, which feels steady, safe, and supportive to those around you.

Principle 1 invokes the power of *trusting* our connection to the sea of energy we live in, and in doing so consciously, we open more fully to new possibilities and discoveries. Principle 2 invokes the power of *feeling* the life force within our bodies, which opens us to the experience of more vitality and joy.

Present Moment Sensory Awareness

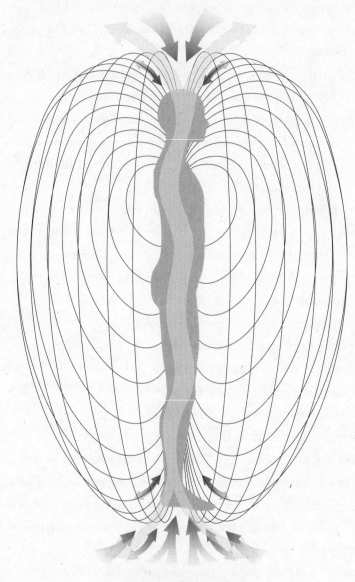

**PRESENT MOMENT
SENSORY AWARENESS**
Full of Energy Flow

Full Body Awareness enables our navigational system to operate optimally, with clear communication among all the parts of ourselves.

Principle 3 invokes the power of *integrating*, of having this unconditional energy source available throughout our entire body, allowing the very cells of the body to absorb nourishing energy. This process creates a stronger flow of energy in the body. From this level of connection, our energy field widens and expands into a strong, integrated presence. More of us is available to enjoy life.

The third principle reminds us that we are meant to have every part of ourselves in communication with every other part and that everything works best when our energy supply is continually replenished. Then we operate in the flow of life. Many of us, however, do not have every part of ourselves participating in this ideal communication, because of traumas, whether physical accidents or emotional traumas, which lock parts of ourselves away or freeze us in a dysfunctional state. Stress, illness, and exhaustion also contribute to the Disrupted Body Presence that is the outcome. Judgment is not helpful here, but the simple recognition that we function best when all parts of our navigational systems are fully operational does help.

I believe our future as a species hinges on whether we can learn to live fully in our bodies, no longer rejecting parts of ourselves as sinful, bad, or dangerous. But this is not easy to do because we can easily be derailed and intimidated in our culture. If we can learn to listen to our inner wisdom, though, we can make of our bodies a strong physical container, from which our souls can create whatever we came here to create.

Invoking our Full Body Presence calls our life force home to us, allowing it to fully inhabit and inspire us. An innate integrity beyond external rules and morality comes into play when we make decisions and create in our world from a more fully integrated self. When we have more energetic awareness in the present moment and listen to all parts of ourselves, whatever decision we make is bound to be wiser than if one part of us dominated our choices. Would you drive a car if one part of the engine were not working? When that happens, it causes other

Sensing Disrupted Energy

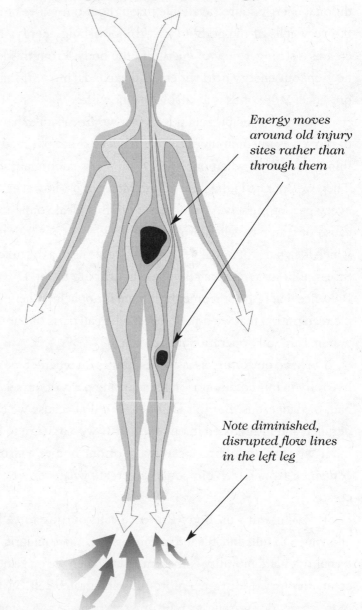

Energy moves around old injury sites rather than through them

Note diminished, disrupted flow lines in the left leg

Growing energetic awareness leads to a heightened ability to sense areas of flow and connection as well as areas of disruption in our internal landscape.

parts of the engine to break down — like driving without enough oil or without all the cylinders firing. Yet we grow up being told not to feel or live in certain parts of ourselves, and then we wonder why we have difficulties when events in life require the wisdom of our blind spots.

When you develop a strong physical container that is flowing with energy, it is easier to be in the present moment. You feel the joy that is here now, and you become strong enough to heal past or hidden traumas without becoming retraumatized or emotionally overwhelmed. Your very presence is healing. A full container gives you a cushion of resilience, which prevents burnout from excessive stress. With healthy boundaries, you more easily protect and support yourself, because you are sure that your needs are being met while still holding your heart open to the world around you.

As your integration expands and deepens, you gain a more intimate sense of your internal road map. You will sense where it is that you have a greater flow of energy and where it is that you have less and are blocked. You will identify your unique energy habits. This deep connection is essential to the entire healing process.

The key to integration boils down to exploring all your emotions, thoughts, and beliefs with curiosity, and to having the courage to let every part of your internal landscape inform you of its wisdom. So, if you have been afraid to explore what's in your heart — how much tenderness you feel there — you can build the trust and courage to go into your heart more fully, rather than defending, rejecting, or protecting yourself from your heart's desires and requests.

Does the container of my being feel good and full of life?

Integration also involves being willing to feel your belly and your pelvis, those foundational areas of power and support in the body. When there is a clear connection and flow of energy from the pelvis and the belly to the heart, the heart is supported and held in a more consistently powerful way. More energy becomes available to create and follow through on your heartfelt desires. This might mean, however, first having the courage to reclaim your pelvis and to stand in your power.

And speaking of standing, when you can fully inhabit your pelvis, feet, and legs, and feel connection with the earth, you can walk in your world connected to healthy resources, with your inner knowing guiding your way. Every part of us, literally every cell, has an innate intelligence, informing us in every moment of what it needs and what it can give to the rest of the body for its health and well-being.

Think of your body as your unique, personal navigational system for inner knowledge and guidance about how to operate optimally in the world. The more fully you can inhabit all aspects of yourself, the more access you have to your inner wisdom and living well. The more access you have to that quiet voice of deep knowing that guides you so beautifully when you can hear it. When you are in your navigational system fully, you know intimately where you are, who you are, and what you need to thrive. You know how to connect when that is desirable and how to hold your boundary when that is appropriate and necessary. And, the fullness of your being enables you to be a strong presence in your life and the lives of those around you, with grace and ease.

PRINCIPLE 4
EXPAND Your Perceptual Lens

Expanding your perceptual lens enables you to see clearly, release expectations and limiting beliefs, and open fully to life.

Our ability to open to life also depends on the width of our perceptual lens. The metaphor of a perceptual lens for how we perceive our world doesn't refer just to our visual perception but also to our sensations, thoughts, beliefs, memories, and dreams. Whenever the lens of the eye is narrowed or distorted, our visual perception is limited or skewed. In the same way, whenever our beliefs, memories, or expectations narrow our perceptual lens, our life experience is limited. When we open to new possibilities or take in new experiences, our perceptual lens naturally expands. It can expand or narrow multiple times in any given day, depending on how we interpret the events and interactions that come our way.

Although our perceptual lens is invisible when it is outside of our conscious awareness, it still forms the background context from which we live our lives. Our perceptual lens is based on our judgments, our interpretation of events, which are filtered through our beliefs, expectations, emotions, and bodily sensations. Because our lens is frequently narrowed in some way, our ability to realize our hopes and dreams, to live an authentic life, and to remain true to ourselves is often severely compromised.

The dominance of the linear mind in our culture makes this principle particularly important. We are prevented from fully experiencing life when we live from our heads and discount our bodily sensations. As we begin to move in a healing direction, one of the first stumbling blocks most of us run into is our narrow perception of ourselves and the world around us. Having internalized the messages delivered so powerfully by our culture, we are hamstrung by its limiting beliefs.

Is my perceptual lens wide enough to recognize my gifts and talents?

Principle 4 invokes the power of *expanding* our perceptual lens so that we can open our mind to different thoughts. We discover there is more to life than we thought when we open ourselves up to the possibilities and quiet the immediate judgment of the mind. Having said that, let's acknowledge that we all compare and judge. At one moment, you may believe someone to be smarter, more evolved, or better than you in some way. Moments later, you may decide that someone else is

Awareness Being Pulled into Past Experiences

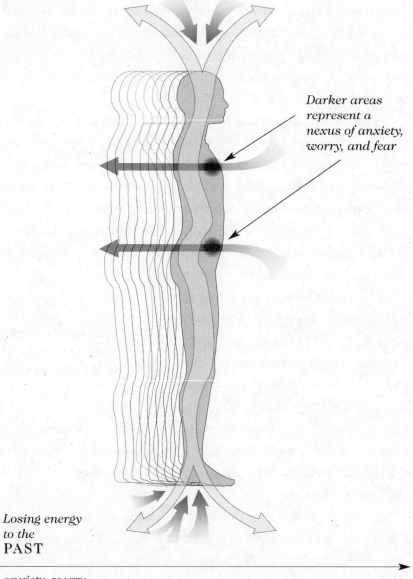

Darker areas represent a nexus of anxiety, worry, and fear

Losing energy to the PAST

anxiety, worry, fear

When conscious or unconscious awareness is pulled into past experiences, traumas, and events, our perceptual lens narrows and prevents us from being fully present.

self-indulgent and too talkative, so that now you feel better than someone. In no time, another incident leaves you feeling less than all over again. These defensive gyrations are expected when seeing life through a narrow lens.

When we see through a narrow perceptual lens, it's because some aspect of our past continues to color our present experience — as well as our outlook on the future. We see through filters that prevent us from fully seeing ourselves and the world as it is in the present moment. So, how do we move beyond this? How do we open our minds, recognize our judgments and limiting beliefs, and invoke this principle of expanding our perceptual lens?

Building on the principles we have already examined — *feeling* inside your body, *trusting* the flow of energy moving through you, and *integrating* the energy throughout the container of your being — you will begin to notice more acutely when your lens has narrowed, when you are caught in a limiting belief. Notice what it feels like in your body when your energy field tightens down around thoughts of hopelessness or despair. Notice how it feels when you think thoughts that require you to maintain a mask or persona that is not really you. These feelings indicate a Disrupted Body Presence, the signature of a narrow perceptual lens.

What judgment or limiting belief comes to mind right now?

Tune in to the tightness or the charge you feel in your body when you pass judgment on someone or something, especially when you're sure you are right and the other person is wrong. What is the sensation in the pit of your stomach when you are feeling you are not good enough in some way? See if you can simply notice these feelings and sensations with as little self-judgment as possible. Noticing in a more neutral, compassionate way creates an opportunity to choose to expand your lens.

Let's look at the steps of this process more closely.

Awareness Being Pulled into Future Possibilities

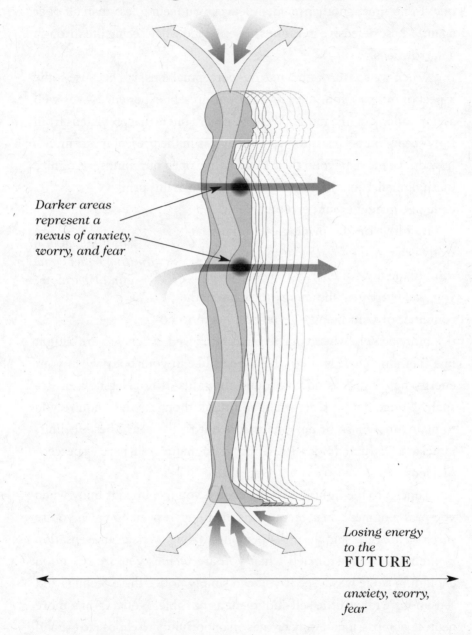

Darker areas represent a nexus of anxiety, worry, and fear

Losing energy to the **FUTURE**

anxiety, worry, fear

When caught in anxiety, worry, and fear about the future, we are pulled out of the present moment, which is energetically draining and narrows our perceptual lens.

1. Become energetically aware of the charge or the tightening in your internal landscape when you see the world in a particular limiting way. Do this without succumbing to the limiting view.

2. Recognize that in this present moment this perception is not necessarily true. Question the validity of the perception, and begin to shake loose its hold on you. After all, you really don't know if it's true or not. The challenge is to try to stay as neutral as you can and not to give credibility to the old voices in your head, which may be reminding you of all the other times you believed you weren't good enough, had failed, and so on.

3. Open to the possibility that there are other ways to perceive yourself and that you can have a more expanded and comfortable experience in your body.

4. Explore what it would feel like in your body, to whatever degree is possible in this moment, if you felt you were good enough. Explore what that would feel like on an emotional and a sensory level. With your body letting go into this new experience, you are also expanding your lens in a powerful and grounded way. You have moved beyond simply thinking about a new way of being to bringing that way of being into your bodily experience. The healing can move throughout your entire system — mind, body, emotions, and spirit.

An anonymous poet offers this good advice on beliefs:

If I continue to believe as I have always believed,
I will continue to act as I have always acted.
If I continue to act as I have always acted,
I will continue to get what I have always gotten.

See Exploration 3, Healing the Internal Resistance to Life, in chapter 7, for examples of how to work with resistance and the tunnel vision of our perceptual lens in many areas of our lives. Knowing how to break the cycle of living from limiting beliefs and becoming open to new sensations and possibilities are what this principle is all about. This principle permeates every area of our lives. When we can practice it regularly, it will set us free.

PRINCIPLE 5

CHOOSE Nourishing Resources Moment to Moment

*Choosing moment to moment to connect
to healthy resources
requires commitment, courage, and kindness;
it provides you with a steady foundation
and a deep sense of inner peace.*

Learning to listen to your body and to tap into healthy resources is an ongoing practice that needs to be embedded in the fabric of your life, into your daily routines and activities. It is important to remember to nourish and nurture yourself, no matter what the situation. The airlines have it right when they tell us to put our own oxygen mask on before assisting those around us. This may require a change in what you pay attention to. If most of your daily attention goes outside of yourself — pleasing and accommodating others or fitting in, even to your detriment — you will need to change this orientation. Balancing your attention inside and outside of yourself will give you a new ability to make healthy decisions. In fact, you may find holding a therapeutic presence for someone else pleasurable and easy when you are listening more to your inner world and nourishing yourself sufficiently.

To begin practicing, choose something small but honestly doable in your life as it is now. After my father died, my mom made sure that she shared one meal a day with someone else in order to stay in contact with the nurturing people in her world. This simple choice helped her stay connected in a way that was easy for her at the time. Nine years later, her network of friends and activities is rich and wide. And it all began with one easy daily step.

Every person is unique; what is nourishing for you may not be nourishing for someone else. Ultimately, only you can know and choose what is most nourishing for you in any given moment. I am reminded of my mom and dad, who found going to an inspiring film a wonderful way to relax and replenish their energy stores. They had entirely different ideas, however, about what makes for an inspiring film. So, they would go to the multiplex cinema together, but each would attend a different inspiring film. They met afterward for tea and sharing. This is an excellent example of holding a healthy boundary — nourishing oneself and having it work well for others too.

What healthy, nurturing resources can help me wake up and begin each day with more energy?

With this book and the audio of Explorations, you are exploring various ways to access a multitude of healthy resources you can choose from, depending on your temperament, as well as your mood and your needs on that particular day. These resources enable you to heal yourself and hold a healing space for others. It is also important to explore the ways in which we lose our sense of connection to life-giving resources, often because of stress, so that we can learn to reconnect and stay connected more of the time.

What healthy resources can nurture me during my workday?

At the heart of this principle is the fact that it is not enough to know *how* to connect to your nourishing resources, because it is paramount also to give yourself permission to make healthy choices on a regular basis. Then the habit grows strong enough to support you when things get stressful. Regular practice, daily if possible, of Exploration 2 is a primary tool for building and maintaining a nourishing energy flow in your body. It is then easier to discern which resources are healthiest and perhaps most pleasurable for you in any given moment. To keep your navigational system fully operational, maintain a solid baseline of energy so you can make better decisions in your life.

It also takes courage to walk your own path of health. Often in our culture, the media bombards us with ways to fill the dreaded emptiness, to numb pain, and to disconnect with a variety of addictions — including excessive shopping, drugs, alcohol, sex, television, Internet surfing. The strategy behind any addiction is avoidance of some part of ourself and the pain or anxiety that comes up with it. Although addictive substances and actions may temporarily ease the pain, ultimately they are life-taking — sucking the energy out of what is healthy, creative, and nourishing in our lives.

Having the presence of mind to choose to refill in a healthy manner, so that you can meet and dissolve pain in life-enhancing ways, means that you are generating new energy habits. These new habits will lead to a lifetime of wellness on many levels. Whenever you start feeling doubtful, fearful, or empty, let those feelings be a signal to you. Let them remind you to feel your feet, to connect to the rich energy of the earth, to take a slow, deep breath, to say a prayer, to take a walk, or to do whatever nurtures and fills you up in a healthy way.

What healthy resources can help me settle down and get a good night's sleep?

Choosing healthy resources from moment to moment is our birthright, and it is always an option. There are all kinds of healthy resources. Here are a few to kickstart your exploration: peacefully resting in your favorite chair, reveling in the warm sun at the beach, hiking in the mountains, feeling a breeze blow through your hair, floating in a pool of water, slowing and deepening your breath, meditating, savoring a quiet cup of tea while your child is at preschool, or calling a good friend to catch up.

One of the most important resources we can choose for ourselves is the nurturing physical touch we looked at in Principle 2. Getting bodywork is one of my favorites. Nurturing touch of all kinds fills me up wonderfully. My system needs different kinds of bodywork, depending on where I am in that moment, but a good massage is always great for slowing down and refilling.

The most valuable healing bodywork for me has been CranioSacral therapy, because it enabled me to heal years of chronic pain and feel more of my body's internal landscape in a pleasurable way. I still return to it regularly to stay clear and healthy in a world full of stress and deadlines. When I forget to schedule regular bodywork sessions or other nurturing experiences, I find myself slipping into working harder than I need to and feeling less energized, with less present moment awareness.

I can learn from my mistakes to make healthier choices.

The other most valuable healthy resource in my life has been movement. Whether it is a good daily walk or a retreat with days of internally inspired movement, I come away feeling juicy and more alive.

Brainstorm your own particular list of things that nurture you in a healthy way. One day it might be to take a long soak in an Epsom salts bath. Another day it might be a long run followed by a sports massage. Another day it might be getting to spend time with good friends, sharing activities that you all enjoy. It could be listening to inspirational music that feeds your soul. Explore new ideas and activities, and keep adding to your list. Be a detective on your own behalf, constantly ferreting out what nurtures you in a *healthy, pleasurable* way.

And, please don't criticize yourself when find yourself feeling disconnected. Be as kind to yourself as you would be to a good friend. Explore the place within that feels disconnected, and hold it with unconditional love. Do this as often as necessary until the sense of separation subsides. In some cases, simply remembering what it feels like to be connected and full is enough. Remember your intention to heal, to reclaim your energy and dreams, and remember the practices that restore you. Do one of them, even if only briefly. Full Body Presence is a moment-by-moment process, which becomes more natural the more you practice it. Eventually, it will be as natural to you as breathing. A sense of steadiness and inner peace will become a part of your daily existence, and you will know you have entered into communion with life itself.

Make a choice now
to notice these principles
when you are in a challenging situation.
Your new awareness can change
both your response
and the outcome.

Chapter Four

The Three Explorations:
The Secrets of This Practice

At the heart of Full Body Presence are the three Explorations on the accompanying audio download or CD. You are encouraged to listen to these repeatedly throughout your work with this book; they are the main tools used to reconnect you with your body and the energy of the universe.

In my twenty-five years of working with these Explorations, I have seen many people use them effectively to facilitate huge transformations. I've seen others struggle with certain elements and walk away before they got what they needed. They didn't fully understand how the process works. This chapter provides critical information for understanding how to get the most out of the Explorations. By reading this chapter before you listen to the audio, you will better understand the concept of Explorations and know the basic guidelines for maximizing your experience.

An important distinction between the Explorations in this book and more traditional guided imagery techniques is that the Explorations are nondirective. They were created, as their name implies, for you to explore your own sensations and feelings, expanding your inner awareness and knowledge. The Explorations do not stipulate a specific outcome or interpretation. They build and refine your sensitivity to your unique internal landscape, and they help you to discern and integrate the connections between your inner and outer worlds.

Experiencing life from inside your body is vital because it is the key to fully inhabiting your world. The body is an incredible navigational system. Almost anyone can take in what's going on around them at a logical, mental level, but if that is the limit of one's conscious level of comprehension, a great deal is being missed. Deepening your sensory experience of who you are inside, at your core, gives you a reliable compass for navigating your life.

The three Explorations are the foundation for this process. Each has a specific purpose, although they are often used in tandem.

Exploration 1. Opening Awareness: Where Am I in This Moment? is designed to help you assess your current awareness of your body. You will be working experientially, listening for subtle cues and sensations that you normally might not notice. You will establish a baseline reading of where you are most present in your body and where you are not as present. Many of my students and clients return regularly to this Exploration to assess the changes life always brings. It serves as a barometer of energy and growing awareness.

Exploration 2. Grounding and Filling: Nourishing and Replenishing the Container of Your Being teaches the all-important concept of understanding and developing your body as a container — a safe, strong vehicle — for your energy and spirit. This is accomplished through a process of staying connected to the rich field of the earth and other healthy resources, while continually filling and replenishing yourself. Use this exercise often, perhaps on a daily basis, to maintain the integrity, strength, and resilience of presence in your body.

Exploration 3. Healing the Internal Resistance to Life helps you to remove the inevitable blocks that come up as you begin to reclaim and energize your whole body. This is the exercise to use whenever obstacles present themselves, such as fear, alienation, confusion, conflict, detachment, negativity, lack of sensation, agitation, disconnection, overwhelm, physical pain, or illness. These issues inevitably surface in our daily lives as we strive to more fully inhabit our bodies. As you explore specific issues with regard to intimate relationships, family dynamics and friendship, work and money, limiting beliefs and personal growth, you can use Exploration 3, in conjunction with Explorations 1 and 2, to help remove those obstacles to healing.

Exploration Guidelines

A separate chapter introduces and explains each of the three Explorations. Each chapter describes the purpose and process of the Exploration, explains the philosophy behind it, and discusses its relationship to the Five Principles of Full Body Presence. The full text of the recorded Explorations can be found in the Appendix at the end of the book.

Our body's internal landscape, as well as the sea of energy around us all, is rich with information and intelligence just waiting to be accessed. All of the Explorations should be done in a relaxed manner. The following guidelines apply to all three Explorations. They will make contact with your inner world easier and help you to hear more clearly what is being conveyed to you at many levels.

Atmosphere and Environment

There are many ways to create an atmosphere and to prepare an environment that will support the Explorations. If you are already familiar with an embodied meditative practice, journaling, or sitting in contemplative prayer, please use what you already know. Add my suggestions where needed. Any practice where you filter out the chatter in the mind first and then listen to the quiet voice within is going to be a good place to start. Explorations are best done in a quiet environment.

Sit in a comfortable chair with good back support. Plant your feet easily and fully on the floor. If your feet don't quite reach the floor, put them on a firm pillow. If you prefer to lie down, bend your knees so that the bottoms of your feet are in contact with the ground. This is not an ideal position because you risk falling asleep when you're horizontal, but it will work in a pinch.

Always feel free to gently move or readjust yourself to remain comfortable throughout the Exploration. You want to be comfortable, relaxed, and, at the same time, awake and aware.

You will find it easiest to travel in your body's internal landscape if you close your eyes and turn your focus within. If you tend to fall asleep when you close your eyes, you can keep them slightly open with a soft focus on something in front of you that won't distract you. The point is to direct your attention inward.

Who Is Driving My Bus?

Our inner worlds are complex, composed of many different parts of ourselves, some long forgotten and others not heard from before. There are ways in which our upbringing and life experiences taught us to deal competently with life's complexity and other ways in which our past experiences have paralyzed us. To exercise some control over the parts of me that are leading at any given time, I use the metaphor of myself as a bus. All the parts of myself are the riders on my bus. When I am feeling down or my inner critic is railing on me, I ask myself, *Who is driving my bus right now?*

When the more integrated, vital parts of me are driving, I am aware of what is going on inside myself and of what is affecting me outside the container of my skin. If I am not aware of what is affecting me, a part of me that I may not have consciously chosen — perhaps my inner critic, anxious self, or a younger, traumatized part — can easily hijack the bus. I may find myself thinking, *I cannot do this, I am a hopeless failure*, or *There must be something wrong with me.* If a grandiose self has hijacked my bus, I may find myself blaming others in order to feel good enough about myself. These parts of ourselves may have served as necessary defenses at some other time in our lives, but they do not help us to realize our dreams and potential now, at this time in our lives. When we become aware of these wayward voices and assertively work with them in the Explorations, we attain mastery in our lives.

So when you find yourself stuck or when judgments come up in any of the Explorations, ask yourself, *Who is driving my bus right now?* Notice what appears in your awareness, without editing or judging. Once you have identified the part of you who is driving, gently but firmly remove it from the driver's seat. My personal tactic is to mentally escort that part of me to the back row of my bus. If it somehow returns to the driver's seat later in the process, I gently and firmly again usher it to the back of the bus. This is a lighthearted and surprisingly effective way to keep thoughts that can derail us at bay. Know that you will likely have to escort these troublemakers to the back of the bus repeatedly. As your work with the Explorations continues, these once unexamined parts of you will lose their power over you. We'll talk more about why this occurs later and offer some effective strategies to meet and disable them.

Put Your Curiosity in the Driver's Seat

The key to overriding our sabotaging inner voices is to invite your curiosity on board. Invite your innate interest in your aliveness to join you in the Explorations. Allow your journey to be playful, not a forced march. Allow your openness to discovery to lead the way. Adopt an openhearted, nonjudgmental attitude, as best you can in that moment. Your experience will be different each time you work with the Explorations. You want to discern what your internal landscape feels like to begin with — with as much openness and as little editorializing as possible. If you notice your judging mind creeping back in as you go along, simply recognize it. Then intentionally remove it from the driver's seat of your awareness. Let a quiet, open curiosity take over again.

No matter who is trying to take control, allow only the part of you that is open to discovery to take the driver's seat of your bus. This aspect of yourself won't second-guess everything you think or do. When it is driving, you'll be inquisitive about and fascinated with life and your internal landscape. Leading with curiosity and openness allows you to have a direct experience of your inner and outer worlds.

By direct experience, I mean an experience that is not colored by interpretation. Direct experience means feeling sensations without immediately attaching mental associations that put the experience in a box or category. It is human nature to judge an experience and immediately categorize it. But if we are deliberate and can catch an experience quickly enough to allow a short time of feeling a sensation in a new way — without interpretation, before habitual associations get attached to it — then we have a chance to experience the world afresh. Fresh eyes give us a wider, more expansive experience, an expanded perceptual lens and access to the present moment. So, whenever you begin work with one of the Explorations, remember to consciously ask your curiosity and openness to drive your bus.

Your Goal Is to Be Here Now

When we are focused on a future goal or expectation, the act of judging whether we've reached that goal or not separates us from the actual experience of the present moment. Judging slows down or halts the process of simply feeling sensation, as our mind kicks in with interpretations of what a sensation might mean or how close we are to our goal. The goal-oriented perfectionist in us has to make an extra effort to shift its focus to cultivating a curiosity about internal sensations from moment to moment.

Full Energy Flow

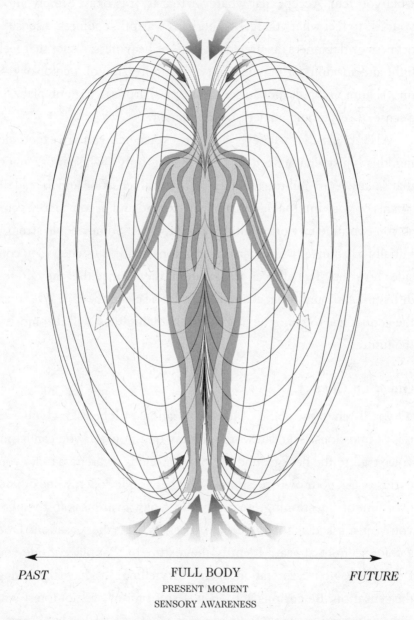

PAST ←————————————————→ FUTURE

FULL BODY
PRESENT MOMENT
SENSORY AWARENESS

When we connect to healthy resources and there are fewer disruptions in our system, energy flows effortlessly through us. This Exploration will feel different every time it is practiced.

By definition, this is an "exploration." The point is to simply notice what you feel. Accept that whatever that is, it is okay. Simply allow yourself to feel what you feel — perhaps warmth, coolness, a sense of dryness or dampness, an area of density or heaviness, a spot that feels light and spacious or maybe empty, the impression of a color or texture, a hum or a pulsation, a soreness or a sharpness, a numb place, or a sense of relaxation, anxiety, or excitement.

Also, know that whatever and however much you are experiencing, this is just what it needs to be. If there is only a whisper of feeling, that's okay. Your abilities to tune in to internal sensation and to read the signals of your internal landscape will expand and become more acute as you continue to work with the Explorations. Some people struggle initially to connect with internal sensations at all. But when they consider how they feel after an Exploration, they notice that they do feel different. Although what changed may not be clear, the shift gives them the confidence to continue practicing, knowing they will feel more in the future.

Question Cues

As you listen to the audio of the Explorations, I'll be asking you a series of questions. You can work with my questions, or you can let my voice trail to the background of your conscious awareness to let your curiosity ask your own questions. Whether you follow my line or your own line of questioning, gently follow your awareness to the place you've just asked about to see what arises. What is the sensation? Does a color seem to appear? Identify the texture of that place inside you. Remember: No interpretation and no storytelling. Just have the feeling, the sensation. Be curious and open. Explorations are not a test with right or wrong answers. Simply notice what you find; what it means will come later.

If your mind wanders or you find yourself spacing out, bring yourself back to the Exploration as soon as you notice. Sometimes this means bringing yourself back over and over throughout the entire process. Don't let this be a problem. Just return your focus to wherever you left off when your mind wandered away. Return to being curious about how you feel inside.

Honor Your Own Natural Process

This is your exploration, so you get to do it in a manner that works for you. If you are highly sensitive, you may need to allow small amounts of sensation at a time, titrating your sensory input, so that you feel comfortable. If you go at your own pace, you can grow your system's capacity to handle more input at some future time. But if you try to rush this — try to get to some self-imposed goal — often your system will close down or stop integrating what you are doing. If at any time during the Exploration you feel uncomfortable or disoriented, open your eyes and reorient yourself, resting until you feel ready to continue. Again, this is not a forced march. Do this at your own pace and in a way that works for you.

After an Exploration

Each time you work with an Exploration, document your experience in some way. You may want to journal, draw, or paint to record your experience. If you are journaling, write down as much of your stream of consciousness of the experience as you can remember. Don't worry about spelling or punctuation — just let language flow out. Giving texture and color to your experience by drawing or painting your internal landscape can be equally valuable. Again, just let it flow out onto the paper. One of my students drew a mandala every day for a year to reflect her Exploration experiences. What emerged was a colorful and beautiful record of her growth and transformation throughout that year.

Another option is to share your experience with another person, or you might speak it into a recording device. One caution: If you are sharing your experience with someone, be sure that person just witnesses and does not try to interpret your experience as you report it.

Engaging in any of these activities right after an Exploration will help your whole system to integrate the experience: right and left brain, color and texture, sound and scent, and other sensations or meanings from the deep unspoken level. Journaling your inner experiences has been shown to accelerate the healing process. So, use any or all of the suggested tools as often as time allows; they will add a whole new dimension to your life and creativity.

*Bring your curiosity and openness
to self-discovery — to your inner landscape.*

Chapter Five

Exploration 1.
Opening Awareness:
Where Am I in This Moment?

*Being willing to listen to our bodies is the first step
in the journey home to ourselves.*

— SUZANNE SCURLOCK-DURANA

These days many of us are busy. For some, the frenzy isn't external as much as it is internal; they find their peace of mind disturbed by a crowd of regrets about the past and worries about the future. Many of us have not been taught how to take a moment to check within ourselves to assess our lives. Cultivating the habit of stopping in the midst of our hustle and bustle, however, to take a few deep breaths and quiet down to listen to our inner voice, centers us in that place inside ourselves that gives us feedback on our feelings, needs, desires, and energy at that moment.

Some people don't even want to know what's going on inside. They just push on, taking care of what needs to be done, ignoring the wisdom of their bodies and the feelings and concerns that are clamoring to be heard. They keep busy, fill every minute, aware on some level that if they slowed down and let themselves feel their inner turmoil, they

would be overwhelmed. And then they might not be able to function —
to work, to take care of the kids, to stay in the relationship or job they
suspect is self-destructive. They do not want to face the long-held
dreams escaping them with every passing day.

Exploration 1 can be thought of as the "check-in" exercise. Its purpose is to give you a framework for stopping and finding out who you
are, what you are feeling, and what you want in this present moment.
It is designed to help you assess your current relationship with your internal landscape. You'll be working experientially, listening for subtle
cues and sensations you might not pay attention to normally. You'll be
taking a baseline reading on your current presence level, noticing where
you feel most present in your body and where you do not.

As you know by now, being in the present moment is everything.
This Exploration can help you move from where you are now to a
deeper, more fully embodied presence, in your inner and outer worlds.
Your present moment awareness will deepen with the Explorations that
follow, but this one is the entrance gate. Without it, we are left thinking about being present but not actually feeling it.

Carol Rediscovers the Wisdom in Her Body

A longtime student of mine recently lost her husband quite suddenly to
a heart attack. In speaking with me throughout the first few months
after his death, Carol shared the following:

> Thank you for this work. I hate to think where I would be without
> the skills to listen to what my body is saying to me, moment by mo-
> ment. The first month was filled with waves of grief, on top of fu-
> neral details, plus all the family expectations heaped on me. I began
> to have serious heart palpitations. My anxiety level was sky-high. My
> internal awareness was minimal at that point. I was busy taking care
> of everyone else.
>
> So I stopped, tuned in, and began to move back in a healthy di-
> rection based on what I was feeling inside. I got my heart checked out

medically. When all the tests came back clear, it dawned on me what was happening. The night of John's death, when I woke up and realized that he was breathing his last breath beside me, I gasped in horror and froze. I have been unconsciously "holding my breath" to some degree ever since. When I checked inside, I realized my diaphragm was clamped down tightly, and the tension in my chest was triggering my palpitations.

By using her internal awareness skills, Carol was able to accurately assess her health situation and take the steps she needed. As she moved through her life from that point forward, she checked in with herself frequently. In doing so, she made important changes. She slowed down the pace of her life and adopted self-care habits again. Carol knew she needed to do whatever it took to start breathing deeply and fully again. She went in for a massage, got some emotional counseling, and talked more things out with friends. As she made her way through this time, she described how her body slowly, day by day, became her friend again. She began to listen to her body as a vital ally, not something to be controlled in order to meet other people's expectations. It was a guide, indicating when it was time to stop, rest, let herself grieve, go for bodywork, care for herself.

Her words to me as we closed our last conversation were, "I know I can do this now. I have the skills I need. My ability to slow down, tune in, and listen really pulled me through. I feel like I have passed a final exam. I would never have asked for this magnitude of a loss to learn this about myself, but now, having done it, I am amazed and grateful." Carol's experience is a wonderful reminder that we have the information we need to heal waiting inside to be discovered, when we slow down and tune in.

Exploration 1 may be used periodically to check in and assess how you are doing, what you are feeling, how you are responding to a particular issue or process. It is a reliable barometer of your level of presence with yourself.

Before you listen to the first Exploration audio, briefly review the keys to unlocking this process.

- Turn your focus inward.
- Invite your curiosity to lead the way.
- Adopt an openhearted, nonjudgmental attitude.
- Give yourself permission to explore.
- Go at your own pace, one that feels comfortable for you.
- Allow yourself to simply feel what you feel.
- If your mind wanders, gently bring it back.
- And enjoy!

*Now that we have set the stage, listen to
Exploration 1 and then return to this page.
(See page 11 for download instructions.)*

After listening to Exploration 1, remember that it is always helpful to augment this work by writing in your journal, drawing, moving, or engaging in any other expressive outlet that captures your experience. The following suggested journal questions may stimulate your thoughts and awareness. Feel free to use them if you find them helpful.

Journal Questions

1. What did you notice that was familiar to you in your internal landscape?
2. What surprised you?
3. If you can, describe any sensations, colors, shapes, textures, vibration levels, or densities that showed up during this experience.
4. What were your dominant thoughts and feelings as you began this check-in?
5. Was there a place in your body where any of those thoughts or feelings were anchored?

6. What places felt frozen or inaccessible, and what thoughts, if any, came up there?

7. What places felt ease or lightness, and what thoughts, if any, came up there?

8. How did any of that shift or change through the course of the Exploration?

9. What stayed the same throughout the Exploration?

10. Did any part of your body's internal landscape inform you of anything you need to take action on in your life?

11. Was anything a puzzle that still needs to percolate within you?

12. How soon would your internal landscape like you to check in again?

Allow yourself to simply feel what you feel.
Stop, tune in, and listen.

Chapter Six

Exploration 2.
Grounding and Filling:

Nourishing and Replenishing the Container of Your Being

Cultivate the root.
The leaves and branches will take care of themselves.

— CONFUCIUS

Stress, tension, overwork, anxiety, worry — these are hallmarks of everyday life for many of us. Sometimes it seems as though we're all driving in the fast lane. These steady pressures accumulate and over time take a stealthy, life-sapping toll on our energies and our ability to cope with our responsibilities. Just as importantly, our ability to take pleasure in our lives is affected. It can easily get to the point where our bodies are so depleted that our minds become muddled. We forget things, or lose things, or find it exhausting to do what we need to do. We are tired and susceptible to illness. Our bodies seems to be letting us down. We have lost our resilience, our ability to bounce back and enjoy life's experiences.

Although the body is perfectly capable of healing itself and restoring our energy, this isn't simply a matter of diet, pills, or taking time off. The body needs to heal from the inside, from the core, and that is the gift of Exploration 2. It takes us on a journey home to ourselves, replenishing and refilling our life force so that we can heal.

Sarah's Health Returns

Daily chronic pain had been a part of Sarah's life ever since her car accident three years before she came to see me. As I treated her old injuries with CranioSacral therapy, her system responded beautifully, but my treatments were not as effective as I knew they could be. She was not sustaining the therapeutic gains made in our sessions.

In our work together, Sarah realized that she was not completely healing from her injuries because she was so busy that she never had any downtime. And when she did take time out, she had no idea how to deeply rest and receive what her body needed. She was always in gear, ready to go, and had been that way all her life. Carrying the load for her family, and doing a great job of it, was the way she had always done things.

Sarah worked with Exploration 2 to learn how to replenish herself. She was amazed at how tired she felt the first time she tuned in to her system. This passed as she gave herself permission to slow down and to receive the nourishing energy her system sorely needed. We brainstormed how she could create resting time for herself every day. She committed to working with Exploration 2 every morning and to building her day's schedule around what her body needed each day.

Initially, it was extremely difficult for Sarah to break the habit of doing it all for her family, not getting the rest she needed in the process. But as the weeks passed, and her lifelong self-discipline became her ally, she gave herself one small self-care item every day. She continued to receive bodywork and did Exploration 2 every morning. Then she discovered that when she did this Exploration in the evenings, it helped her sleep. Within several months, as the treatments held, Sarah's pain completely disappeared. She had more energy for her life and her family. When we last spoke, she told me that she still used Exploration 2 at bedtime, because it reliably helped her relax and get a better night's sleep. This, of course, gave her more energy for the next day.

Sarah's experience reminds us that sometimes healing is a matter of changing how we see ourselves and opening to the simple, yet profound, process of connecting to an unconditional healthy resource and allowing it to fill and nourish us. I call this process of replenishing and strengthening the body "grounding and filling." As its name indicates, this Exploration will help you learn how to ground yourself more firmly on the earth and open to absorb its nourishing energy, filling your body from feet to head and from your core to the boundaries of your skin. Over time, grounding and filling will heal and fortify areas of pain, numbness, weakness, or emotional distress.

Not only is this process vital for healing and daily vitality, it is also extremely valuable in times of acute stress, panic, and even danger. Exploration 2 helps us to become a strong, steady presence, better able to bring all of ourselves and our resources to bear in any given situation.

Lisa in Danger

Several months after taking my basic course, Lisa awakened to a man with a gun standing over her bed where she and her boyfriend had been asleep. Her report of what happened follows:

> He was jumpy and skittish, and I was initially terrified that he was going to impulsively strike out and shoot us. He tied us together in the bed and left us in the dark, telling us he would be back for us. My boyfriend froze, but I remembered your words and began to ground myself and use the calming breath you taught us. When the robber came back into the room a few minutes later, I talked to him calmly and clearly, asking him what he was looking for and giving him directions to find what he wanted. As I continued to ground myself and we talked, he became less agitated. I calmly asked him not to hurt us and told him we would give him what he needed. He quieted down even further, as I continued to ground and fill — all the while

tied up in my bed! Several times he left us and returned. Eventually, he left the house, leaving us unharmed.

Given his initial agitation and instability, I honestly don't know if I would be alive today if I hadn't had that training. Staying grounded and steady probably saved us. I wouldn't ever want that to happen again, but I do now know that I can stay steady, grounded, and present, even under the direst of circumstances. I think this skill is vital for dealing with the uncertainty and trauma so pervasive in these times.

Exploration 2 is the foundation process for healing yourself. It is a satisfying and rejuvenating process that provides a steadiness in the body that no one can take from you. I encourage you to take the time out for yourself to do it as often as possible, ideally every day, to strengthen and nourish your body's internal landscape. Do this so that you can receive what you need for your own healing, so that you can take care of your own needs and responsibilities. Ultimately, you find yourself able to be fully present to the needs of others without feeling overburdened or burned out. In fact, once you have built up your inner resources and established strong boundaries to contain the energy, you will have plenty for yourself and those you love.

Before you listen to Exploration 2, briefly review the keys to unlocking this process:

- Turn your focus inward.
- Invite your curiosity to lead the way.
- Adopt an openhearted, nonjudgmental attitude.
- Give yourself permission to explore.
- Go at your own pace, one that feels comfortable for you.
- Allow yourself to simply feel what you feel.
- If your mind wanders, gently bring it back.
- And enjoy!

Now that we have set the stage, listen to Exploration 2 and then return to this page. (See page 11 for download instructions.)

After you have listened to Exploration 2, it can be helpful to augment your experience by writing in your journal, drawing, moving, or engaging in any other expressive activity that captures your experience. The following suggested journal questions may stimulate your thoughts and awareness. Feel free to use them if you find them helpful.

Journal Questions

1. What did you notice that was familiar to you in your internal landscape?
2. What surprised you?
3. If you can, describe any sensations, colors, textures, shapes, vibration levels, or densities that showed up during your experience.
4. What were your dominant thoughts and feelings as you began this check-in?
5. Was there a place in your body where any of those thoughts or feelings were anchored?
6. How did any of that shift or change through the course of the Exploration?
7. What stayed the same throughout the Exploration?
8. Did any part of your internal landscape inform you of anything you need to take action on in your life?
9. Was anything a puzzle that still needs to percolate within you?

*When you are grounded and full,
you are strong and steady.*

Chapter Seven

Exploration 3.
Healing the Internal Resistance to Life

*People say that what we are all seeking is a meaning for life.
I don't think that's what we are really seeking. I think that
what we're seeking is an experience of being alive, so that
our life experiences on the purely physical plane will have
resonances within our own innermost being and reality, so
that we can actually feel the rapture of being alive.*

— JOSEPH CAMPBELL

After working with Explorations 1 and 2, you are probably feeling stronger, more confident, more resilient, and capable of facing both life's demands and your own desires. You are probably more aware of the problems and deficits in your life, and you may be less willing to simply tolerate them. But what can you do? The thought of making changes or demands — requesting more time with your partner, setting healthy boundaries with your child, asking for a deserved raise — makes you nervous and queasy, maybe even paralyzes you.

Whenever we are consciously waking up and becoming more energized, there is a part of us that is afraid to take the next step, the step that brings us into more aliveness. The word for this feeling is "resistance." It surfaces when we want to do something beyond our comfort zone, something outside our known world. Resistance is different from having a healthy boundary and saying "no" when something is not right for us. Resistance is that part of us that is afraid to move forward; it says "never," "I can't," or "I shouldn't." Many of our unhealthy and unproductive behaviors originated as a means of self-protection. We learned to withhold our opinions, do what we were told, follow an acceptable career path, marry an acceptable partner, keep our anger under wraps or use it as a shield, dress in a way that doesn't draw attention — the list goes on and on.

Until we start to wake up, to explore what's inside us, we hardly notice we are living by rules that stifle us. Often our rules are keeping us from getting what we want in our lives. Although they once served us well, or at least allowed us to get by under the circumstances in which they originated, they may well now be outdated or even self-destructive.

Even so, we often cringe at the thought of the possible consequences of change, convinced that we will suffer the loss of those we love and what is familiar. It's the normal human reaction, and it can exert a tight hold on us. And yet, for all the initial resistance, the more we explore our internal landscape, the more we come to crave that sense of full aliveness. In fact, moving through resistance can lead to a breakthrough experience of Full Body Presence.

This chapter is about facing and overcoming resistance. It discusses the many forms resistance can take and then moves right into Exploration 3 — a powerful internal alchemical process for working with all forms of resistance. Chapter 8 shares anecdotes and case histories to illustrate situations in which resistance arises, and offers guidelines for tailoring the Exploration to address the places where resistance arises in different areas of your life.

Masquerade

Resistance has many faces. Most of us are well aware of some of the ways in which resistance shows up — those areas in our lives where we are afraid to move forward or are habitually gripped by some emotion that stops us, such as a fear of public speaking or a fear of heights. Other aspects of our resistance are more subtle and less conscious, such as resistance to receiving love or praise or to living fully in our power.

Our resistance often takes the form of somatic symptoms. These may include chronic physical distress, which can manifest as tight muscles or painfully restricted motion in different parts of the body. Such parts of us are rigid, frozen, numb, or in pain. Of course, not all pain or physical blockage is the "face of resistance," but this is often the case.

One of my clients, Robert, came in complaining of tight muscles and painful restricted motion in his neck and shoulders. His shoulders stooped, as though he were carrying the proverbial weight of the world. Robert was having a great deal of difficulty in his job. He had been receiving negative feedback, which undermined his confidence. His boss's criticism launched Robert into childhood memories of his critical father and Robert's powerlessness to stand up to him. The paralysis in his current job and the pain in his neck were directly connected to Robert's resistance to acknowledging the fear that he wasn't good enough for the job — similar to the feeling Robert had as a child who would never be good enough for his father.

After working with all three Explorations over a period of several weeks, Robert came to realize that his neck and shoulder pain were directly connected to his early fears, which had completely overwhelmed and paralyzed him as a child. He recognized that his current physical symptoms were his body's resistance to feeling that fear again. The pain subsided and the normal motion in his neck returned, however, as he was able to meet that fear and resolve it. He was freeing himself up to take action at work, to speak up and rebut the negative feedback and to resolve the issues he was facing there.

It's All Your Fault

Underneath the more conscious faces of resistance is a deeper kind, one we all have difficulty recognizing and owning up to. This resistance we blindly project out onto the world around us, misguidedly blaming someone else or circumstances for the distress we feel inside. Even though our projection is unconscious, its effects in our lives — and the lives of those around us — can be quite powerful and destructive.

Sometimes it takes me weeks just to identify this kind of resistance as mine before I can begin to take responsibility for it, face it, and work with it. The more honestly I explore my internal landscape, the quicker this awareness can rise to my consciousness. For example, when I am having a heated disagreement with my husband and I am fully convinced of how right I am, I eventually realize that I am projecting my own stuff onto him. Then I know I need to look deeper to see how I am really feeling underneath all that self-righteousness.

If you are married or partnered with someone, one of the easiest places to project your resistance is onto your partner. It happens in the blink of an eye. Suddenly your internal anxiety, fear, rage, shame, distress, or sense of disconnection no longer have anything to do with you. It can sound like this: "I would feel happier, more alive, more content if only my partner were more loving, emotionally honest, sensitive, a better provider, or less rigid, controlling, obsessive, or smothering." In this case, the disruption in your energetic awareness comes from focusing your attention outside yourself.

When you see your partner through this narrowed perceptual lens, a part of your aliveness process comes to a screeching halt while you wait for something outside yourself to change. You have unknowingly given your power away. When you take back the reins of responsibility for your own happiness, your power returns as well. No matter what the outcome, how you feel about it changes completely when you are holding the reins of your own life.

If you are not married or partnered, this dynamic looks just slightly different. The cast of characters changes, perhaps to your perceived selfish friend, an unappreciative boss, or a controlling parent. Remember that in these examples, I am pointing out underlying patterns in the ways we judge ourselves and the world and then unconsciously project these judgments. The surface content of a pattern will look different in new situations, but you are likely mixing and matching your personal collection of deeper behavior patterns.

If Only

Another common form of resistance is to secretly, or not so secretly, wait for the someone or something of one's dreams to come along to finally make one whole and truly happy. This behavior pattern shows itself in various forms — a fear of rejection, impossibly high standards, a fear of commitment or of entrapment, for example. In whatever form, this pattern limits us because we disconnect from our internal experience and dissipate our energy focusing outside ourselves, looking for that other person or situation that is going to solve our internal distress or loneliness. In this pattern, we once again unknowingly relinquish our power. When we stop waiting and we take back the responsibility for our happiness, our power returns as well. Opportunities come to us when we are at home in our power, open to receive what we desire.

It's a Cold, Hard World Out There

And then there are those of us who, based on a past painful experience, decide the world is indeed not a safe place for our heart. We then choose the easiest and least painful route to a sense of well-being: we close off the vulnerable parts of ourselves and compensate for this in some other way. But the end result is that we lose internal connection with ourselves by believing our fearful projections about the external world. It's not that we haven't had real experiences that created the basis for our perceptions and projections; it's that our decisions about those events were made while looking through a narrowed and now outdated lens. Once again, energy loss will naturally occur when we close off a part of ourselves in this way.

The most extreme form of resistance, addiction, is the most difficult to recognize clearly because of its hallmark of denial. All addictions — from excessive drinking, eating, gambling, shopping, working, to Internet surfing, or even excessive exercising — are ways to escape painful or unacceptable internal sensations. Even milder forms of addiction, such as overscheduling your life or procrastination, serve the same purpose. And denial alone, with or without an addiction, is in itself a powerful form of resistance. We all have parts of ourselves and our lives that we don't feel comfortable acknowledging and owning, but we need to remember that when unacknowledged, they are likely at the root of any Disrupted Body Presence we are experiencing.

Can You See the Forest for the Trees?

When we can stand back a bit from our problems to see from a broader perspective, it becomes clear that the underlying cause of much of our resistance boils down to one cause: our beliefs. Our beliefs about ourselves and the world are, for the most part, handed down to us from our families, communities, and culture. Not knowing any better, we blindly accept and internalize these, but our narrow, hand-me-down beliefs limit the perceptual lens through which we view the world.

It is important to keep in mind that no matter what our issue or problem seems to be, it is not likely that we are seeing it "as it is." Our unexamined narrow view is selectively closed off to people and places, concepts and opinions, ideas and solutions that don't fit within the scope of our lens. We cannot see what we cannot conceive of or what we reject. Exploration 3 guides us to recognize and let go of limiting beliefs so that we can see more clearly. It shows us how to discover and nurture a place of well-being and strength within ourselves that enables us to feel safe. Feeling safe, we can trust more, and trust helps us to expand our perceptual lens.

Exploration 3 addresses all forms of resistance. You can use it to resolve issues and disconnections in interpersonal relationships or to resolve internal issues and disconnections — down to the most microscopic, cellular, molecular, DNA levels. As you begin to heal your inner fear, denial, and disconnection, outer situations of fear and disconnections or fearful situations lose their power over you. The emotional charge involved in placing your center of well-being on others — or external situations — dissolves. You no longer lose energy to your outer world. You regain your internal power to choose.

This means that if your spouse or boss is actually abusive in some way, or some other change needs to be made in your world, you now have a clear head and an effective voice with which to act. You are empowered. You can see what choices you need to make to resolve the situation, and the path unfolds from there. This makes this Exploration an excellent adjunct to therapy of any kind: from couples counseling or individual psychotherapy to bodywork. You can enhance the therapeutic outcome of any healing session when you go into it as an internally informed, empowered person.

How Is This Done?

Let's look at how we can successfully resolve obstacles and resistance to our natural energy flow. What practical steps can we take to reclaim this sense of connectedness within ourselves? Our natural state of being is one of interconnectedness with all aspects of ourselves, even though we may have inadvertently or consciously pushed away some aspects, put others to sleep, and judged ourselves and the world, creating a false sense of separation.

The foundation for Exploration 3 is laid by the strong container Exploration 2 creates, when grounding and filling, as well as the opening awareness Exploration 1 cultivates. I suggest that before proceeding with this session, you go back and repeat the first two Explorations (over as many days or weeks as needed) until you feel comfortable with the process of filling and energizing yourself and feeling your body as a container for your energy.

Next, choose to work with a straightforward instance of physical resistance or distress for your introduction to this exercise. In the future, you can use Exploration 3 to address more complex or seemingly intractable problems. The key here is to be gentle, kind, and persistent with yourself. With regular practice of this Exploration, you will continually be moving in the direction of connection and integration. With each round of this exercise, as you gently reestablish contact with that core place more deeply, you will feel less disconnected. Trust that you are letting these layers go at a pace that is just right for you.

Although this process cannot be rushed, when the moment is right, integration can take place in an instant. It can happen that when you repeat this Exploration, addressing a particular area of your resistance, suddenly the last layer dissipates or transforms, and you experience a wonderful rush of energy and deep connection. Your natural energy flow is fully restored. When this occurs, even if it comes quietly, there's no missing it.

It is important that throughout this Exploration, you allow yourself to truly meet the place, or places, inside yourself where you feel a disconnection. As easy as this may sound, most of us cannot do this ourselves. We may hover around a spot, getting to know each curve and corner of the edges of our resistance, but to actually connect with it is a rare and profound experience — particularly if we are engaging a place of chronic physical or emotional pain.

The energy that truly allows the alchemy of deep transformation to occur is love — "love" in the sense of "agape," the ancient all-encompassing, unconditional love of God, Goddess, Christ, Buddha, Great Spirit, or any other name given to the compassionate source of life. Agape brings us into a deep connection with the Universe. Again, allow yourself to deeply feel this love in your body, not simply to imagine or visualize it (although it may have visual components). The energy of love ignites the alchemy of true healing, transforming tight, painful, wounded places into connected, healed components of who we are. When this alchemy is complete, out of our deepest wounds can come our greatest gifts.

Exploration 3 has three segments. You may stop after any of the three segments or go all the way through. The first segment explores a physical place of resistance, the second addresses limiting beliefs and painful recurring thoughts, and the third segment facilitates the healing of relationships. They are in this order because they build on each other. You will be given the option to stop the session at the end of each segment (which is signaled by a ten-second period of silence) or to continue through the entire Exploration. Remember, we all work at our own pace, and this process cannot be rushed.

The starting point for this Exploration is a strong foundation of healthy sensation in your body. Sit quietly now for a minute or two and identify an area of physical distress or discomfort. If you don't know what to choose right now, let it go; in the audio session, you will be given clear guidance on how to find a good spot. The truth is that wherever we are on the path, we all have resistance to whatever our next step is. Fortunately, as we practice these Explorations, each step along the way gets easier and easier to take.

Now...

- Turn your focus inward.
- Invite your curiosity to lead the way.
- Adopt an openhearted, nonjudgmental attitude.
- Give yourself permission to explore.
- Go at your own pace, one that feels comfortable for you.
- Allow yourself to simply feel what you feel.
- If your mind wanders, gently bring it back.
- And enjoy!

Now that we have set the stage, listen to
Exploration 3
and then return to this page.
(See page 11 for download instructions.)

After you have listened to Exploration 3, you may find it helpful to augment your process by writing in your journal, drawing, moving, or engaging any other expressive outlet that captures your experience. The following suggested journal questions may stimulate your thoughts and awareness. Feel free to use them if you find them helpful.

Journal Questions

1. What did you notice that was familiar to you in your internal landscape?
2. What surprised you?
3. If you can, describe any sensations, colors, textures, shapes, vibration levels, or densities that showed up during this experience.
4. What were your dominant thoughts and feelings as you began this check-in?
5. Was there a place in your body where any of those thoughts or feelings were anchored?
6. How did any of that shift or change through the course of the Exploration?
7. What stayed the same throughout the Exploration?
8. Did any part of your internal landscape inform you of anything you need to take action on in your life?
9. Was anything a puzzle that still needs to percolate within you?

Allow yourself to truly meet a place inside where you feel a disconnection. Although this sounds simple, the experience is profound.

Chapter Eight

Using the Explorations and the Five Principles for Integration and Renewal

The anecdotal stories and case histories in this chapter have been chosen to reflect a broad spectrum of issues relating to the everyday challenges people experience. What you will read includes personal accounts from people who used the Explorations alone, as well as those who had hands-on support during their healing process.

The stories are arranged by principle, because for all these people, one of the Five Principles was the entryway to the core of their challenge. Time and time again, I have witnessed people using one of the principles as a first step that led them to their ultimate healing. After opening that first door, they often use the other principles and Explorations to go deeper and to ensure that the healing they experienced lasts.

Many nuggets of wisdom, from a therapists and a client's perspective, are included here in the follow-up discussions about resonance, relationship, power, and presence. Even if the problem or the issue is not one you are currently experiencing or have experienced in the past, the suggestions may nonetheless be helpful in other ways.

At the end of the stories, specific suggestions illustrate how you might use or adapt one or more of the Explorations to meet your own needs. With practice and familiarity with the process, you will easily be able to refocus an Exploration's version on the audio to reflect the specifics of an issue you are working on. And remember that Exploration 3 has three segments — one for the physical place of resistance in your body, one for limiting beliefs, and another for interpersonal relationship issues.

PRINCIPLE 1
TRUST the Existence of Nurturing Life Energy

Trusting that there is an unlimited source of nourishing, life-giving energy in the Universe allows you to relinquish fear, live from trust, and recognize that you are loved and supported throughout your life.

The following two examples relate experiences in which the principle of trust was the beginning for the healing and integration process. Although other principles are included in these stories, the principle of trust opened the door in both these cases.

My Marriage Is a Disaster

Linda came in to see me when she was feeling hopeless after a separation from her husband. Her abusive, alcoholic husband had been an unhealthy connection in her life for years. She had fallen in love with him when she was young, and she calibrated her worth by his judgments of her. After months of quiet contemplation, Linda had been able to arrive at the decision to end her marriage. However, within days of her decision, she fell prey to fears of being on her own, even though deep inside she knew it was the right move. Linda feared not being able to make it alone, losing herself without a connection to anyone, and succumbing to depressive feelings that tugged at her core. She had worked with a psychotherapist and recognized intellectually what she needed to do in order to move beyond her fears. Despite this work, she continued to feel torn inside — at times depressed, almost suicidal. Linda had lost sight of her trust and the inner wisdom that she could be supported in this decision.

In our first session, we worked with Exploration 1, Opening Awareness, so that she could begin to experience her internal landscape and trust her inner wisdom. As I sat with her, she closed her eyes, took her awareness inside her body, and began to identify where in her body she felt the source of her depression. As she listened closely, it became clear that something was coming from a tightly coiled place in her belly. Inside the tight coil, she was able to identify a part of her that still felt like the abused child she had once been. As she reconnected with this child part of herself, it expressed the feeling that she was not good enough and not strong enough to survive in the world alone. The small child within told her that even though her marriage was a disaster, it was at least a connection. As she listened to the voice of this child-self, she knew it was the source of her doubt about her ability to create new, healthier relationships and to let go of the unhealthy ones.

As I listened, I realized that this fearful part of Linda had long ago lost touch with the healthy support available to her. Her ability to trust in any support was minimal. In response to this, I consciously strengthened my therapeutic presence for her to energetically connect with and receive when she was ready. I did this by relaxing more fully in my own body while maintaining our connection. I used my energetic awareness to check in with how my spine felt against the chair I was seated in. I then dropped my attention to my lower back and legs. I continued to ground and fill, feeling the stability of the earth beneath my feet as we worked. I let my Full Body Presence expand and create a soft, noninvasive cushion of energy to help Linda feel safe and supported. As I did this, I found myself feeling better as well.

Next, Linda looked inside for a place where she felt some sense of connection to her inner strength. She described a presence in her heart, a sense of a "clearheaded woman," who was a source of strength to her. Although Linda had discussed this aspect of herself with her psychotherapist, she had not actually felt this aspect or its power to help her move forward in her life. I gently asked her a series of questions that guided her to perceive how she could connect to healthy resources and receive external support for the clearheaded woman in her heart.

"What sensation, from the rich energy field of the earth, would feel most nourishing coming in through your feet and legs?" We sat quietly, and I grounded with Linda as she began to feel some sensation in her feet and legs, which moved up into her torso.

Next, I asked, "Can you feel a sense of nurturing from the warmth of the sunlight pouring in through the window behind you onto your back?" This healthy resource was indeed palpable for Linda. She immediately began to feel the back of her neck and her rib cage relaxing and spreading out. Soon, she noticed that her chest area was beginning to fill with a warm, tingling sensation, which spread down to her belly and met the warmth coming up from her legs. Linda had systematically accessed two external resources: the feeling of the earth's steadiness coming into her feet and legs and the sensation of gentle warmth coming from the sunlight on her back. Once she felt connected and filled throughout her whole body by these healthy resources, I asked Linda to notice how the clearheaded woman in her heart was feeling in relation to the little girl self. Linda said that the woman felt huge and strong and that the abused little girl felt quiet and peaceful because she had made her way into the arms of the strong woman in her heart. She described her physical body as though it were vastly wider and deeper than her actual physical boundaries. Linda was experiencing Full Body Presence.

She felt very aware of all parts of herself and was delighted that she did not need to exclude any of them despite their intense feelings. All of Linda's emotions and feelings were honored and given expression. Her core wisdom and her fear were both heard and nurtured by the connections inside and outside herself. I recognized that Linda's navigational system was operational again — perhaps for the first time in her adult life.

Linda ended the session with a deeper understanding of her situation. By learning to trust that healthy resources are all around her and to recognize several of them in our session, she was able to fill up the container of her being, which gave her a sense of Full Body Presence she had never had before. From there, healing and integration naturally occurred as her inner wisdom was empowered to act on her behalf. Her perceptual lens expanded to include new possibilities she had never experienced before.

Linda walked away from the session knowing she could self-catalyze this process again if necessary by choosing life-giving resources, rather than falling back into old self-sabotaging habits. As long as we live and walk on the planet, these kinds of healthy resources are always available to us. After the session, Linda continued to work with Exploration 2, grounding and filling herself on a daily basis. This kept her in close contact with her body's internal landscape and able to navigate through her world feeling more connected to her Full Body Presence.

Linda's experience reminds us all that we can access our inner wisdom, nourish ourselves with what we need, and create an intimate and strong relationship with ourselves on all levels.

Specific Suggestions

Learning to Trust the Existence of Nurturing Life Energy was the doorway for Linda. Know that your entry point may differ. If you are someone who knows what you should be doing to lead a healthy and fulfilling life, but something inside consistently sabotages your desires and keeps you from taking actions in a healthy direction, the following suggestions may be valuable:

1. Start by listening to Exploration 1 with an intention to discern where your internal awareness is calling you. Notice what emotions or feelings may be there.

2. When the emotions or sensations are fully present, wait for a belief or an image to emerge, which will guide you to the principle that will be your doorway into deeper discovery. Let your navigational system lead you.

3. Use Explorations 2 and 3 to facilitate uncovering and releasing trapped traumatic energy and limiting beliefs, both of which can prevent you from healing.

4. Repeat all three Explorations as needed, particularly if the patterns are lifelong or deeply imprinted. In this case, the process is best done slowly and in layers, to minimize the potential for overwhelm, and to better integrate the healing. Often, it is most effective to deal with long-standing issues with the help of a grounded facilitator of some kind.

I Lost My Job after Years of Devoted Service

One of my longtime students, Stefan, told me about a time when he was suddenly dismissed from a job he had worked for many years. He was devastated; his usual competent presence was completely disrupted. Stefan felt as though all his hard work had gone unseen and unappreciated; consequently, his self-esteem was at an all-time low. He felt all alone in the fear that he was somehow fundamentally flawed. Hours passed since his dismissal, and though Stefan knew he should move on or take some restorative action, he was still in shock. He believed that this dismissal meant he was a total failure. He knew it wasn't rational to feel this way, but he could not shake it. Stefan was paralyzed by the incident.

Then a friend's chance phone call reminded him of the first principle, Trusting the Existence of Nurturing Life Energy. When Stefan remembered to trust that he could be supported, he realized he didn't have to carry this abysmal event alone. This helped him to break through his wall of painful isolation and speak to his friend truthfully about how he was feeling. In doing this, Stefan allowed his friend to know what was really happening for him rather than leading his friend to believe that everything was okay. His friend's capacity to listen with an open heart offered Stefan a therapeutic presence to connect with. Stefan chose a healthy resource for himself rather than staying mired in the shock of the dismissal. When the call was over, Stefan noticed he felt a little better. He had shared honestly with his friend, and with that he started to refill. From there, he remembered Exploration 2 and tuned in further to ground and fill, connecting to his internal landscape and nourishing himself as best he could in that moment.

Remembering to trust the existence of nurturing life energy, even when he was having a difficult time feeling it, was Stefan's doorway into gathering other healthy resources. For example, he remembered that someone he admired greatly had been through a similar situation and had bounced back with more strength and success than ever. In fact, this admired mentor had used the situation to make a major career change. Stefan imagined what his mentor would do and how he would act if he were in Stefan's current situation. He said it was almost as though his "admired someone" was right there in the room brainstorming with him.

Expanding his perceptual lens was the next doorway in Stefan's healing process. Ideas began to pop into his awareness, as he opened to new ways of looking at his situation. He also called other friends and colleagues who reminded him of his strengths, expanding Stefan's lens on himself even more. By the end of the day, the aching and numbness in his gut had faded. He was able to feel the ground under his feet again and his steadiness was returning. He knew he had the resources and that he could find his way to new possibilities from there.

As the weeks passed and he explored new potential jobs, Stefan used Exploration 3 as a resource. Whenever the remnants of numbness and aching, or the limiting belief that he was somehow fundamentally flawed, would show up, Stefan used them as a signal to stop, tune in, and use Exploration 3 to release and resolve the next layer. Slowly, he regained his Full Body Presence. He felt more and more nurturing energy in his body and integrated this life-giving energy throughout his entire system. It became easier for him to discern and choose the resources that would keep him on track and moving toward his full potential. His confidence in his skills and abilities became stronger every day.

Stefan now has a new job, one that suits him better and in a much healthier work environment. He is using his creativity and talents in a more satisfying way. Stefan has learned to choose resources that keep him connected to his deep strength and steadiness, and he knows that he has the resilience to bounce back and end up in an even better place.

Specific Suggestions

Trusting the Existence of Nurturing Life Energy was the first step for Stefan. Notice that he then proceeded to expanding his perceptual lens and moved through the rest of the principles. This naturally happens in many circumstances, and all you need to do is recognize one of the principles to catalyze the process. Recall that your entry point may differ.

If you have recently experienced a devastating event, it may have triggered one or more of your most crippling, limiting beliefs. This is not unusual. Limiting beliefs are neither rational nor reasonable. They are usually rooted in your past and completely outdated, but nonetheless they can seriously disrupt your presence. The following suggestions may be of help:

1. If you are trapped in a limiting belief, a helpful first step is to stop. Then tune in, and ground and fill. Imagine that your best

friend, a trusted mentor, or another knowledgeable and loving figure is right there with you in the room.

2. Imagine this person in a situation similar to yours. From financial devastation or a sudden breakup to the loss of a job or position and the death of a loved one, we all experience these things at different times.

3. Allow yourself to brainstorm with this person, as Stefan did, how to find a way out of the difficulty.

4. Identify which principle is your first step and which Exploration would be most beneficial to begin healing.

Alternate Suggestions

1. An alternative is to imagine that your best friend or a good client is stuck in the dilemma you are experiencing. What counsel would you provide?

2. How could your friend or client expand his or her perceptual lens to see this issue differently?

3. Would this person believe the limiting belief that you feel stuck in? What would he or she say to move beyond it? Can you say that to yourself?

4. How would this person solve the issue at hand? What principle could be used? Which Exploration would be most beneficial?

To Explore Further

1. Who in your world can you actually reach out to at this time to help you expand your perceptual lens? Can you reach them by phone or in person? Perhaps write them an email or a letter, asking for what you need.

2. Be proactive. Clearly say that you need help moving beyond a specific limiting belief. For instance, if you're going through a breakup and are feeling unlovable and not good enough, ask your friend to help you beyond this limiting view. Despite the mistakes

you made to contribute to the breakup, you first need to get your full container back so that you can see the situation and hear the feedback more clearly. Connect to resources that will refill you.

3. Utilize all the Explorations to get the navigational system of your being up and fully operational again, to recover your Full Body Presence.

Trusting the Existence of Nurturing Life Energy is a key feature in healing and creating what we want in our lives.

As you can see from these examples, trust can be invoked even when the feeling of trust is not there yet. Whatever way you can get in the door and move toward being able to feel that trust is ultimately helpful and life-giving. From this principle, all the other principles of choosing, feeling, integrating, and expanding easily follow.

Notice that the examples and suggestions that follow these two stories are different. One involves learning to trust within yourself, and the other is reaching to external resources that help initiate the feeling of trust. Stefan began his healing process by reaching out, but Linda was led within initially to heal her disruption.

PRINCIPLE 2
FEEL the Presence of Life Energy in Your Body

Feeling your internal connection to life energy
as a natural state of being opens your awareness
to discover a sense of belonging, reclaim your inner wisdom,
and experience vitality and joy.

The following three stories relate experiences where the principle of Feeling the Presence of Life Energy in Your Body was the entryway to healing and integration. Other principles are also at play in these stories, but feeling opened the door in each case.

Feeling My Tumor

Ben has always been a concrete, left-brained kind of guy. When he first arrived in my office, he was only there because someone he trusted referred him. He had recently undergone surgery to remove a completely encapsulated, nine-pound cancerous tumor from his abdomen. This fit man had not noticed there was anything wrong until the tumor was almost full size.

As Ben's story unfolded, it became clear that he had a touch deficit, which left him with a limited capacity to feel much internally below his neck. Growing up in an affluent family, he was given to the care of a nursemaid, who neglected him and gave him very little touch. Memories of hours alone in his crib left Ben numb.

I knew we had to begin by helping him learn to sense his body's internal landscape. Because he doubted himself in this area, at the very start, Ben had to work on suspending judgment of what he was capable of feeling. At first, he had to imagine he could feel inside himself. We played a lot with how different parts of him felt compared with other parts — *Does it feel more dense in your chest or your belly?* — until Ben realized he was capable of sensing his internal landscape. In fact, he could feel quite a lot.

Ben worked with Exploration 1, Opening Awareness, and Exploration 2, Grounding and Filling, a number of times until he began to have a lot more sensation. After one particular grounding and filling, he asked me, "Is it possible that bringing in nourishing energy could regrow my tumor?" When I asked him what he felt during the Exploration, he said that he sensed a tiny nub of a growth in his gut where the other tumor had been removed. I suggested that he could be sensing something important and that he might want to see his oncologist to get it checked out. Indeed, there was a nub of growth, and they went back in and surgically removed the tiny bit of tumor before it could become a problem. Ben was ultimately reassured to know he could feel that keenly — and stay healthy! His ability to feel his internal landscape increased; his ability to trust his energetic awareness increased as well.

Ben used Exploration 3 to hold his gut area with his internal energy hands in an unconditional loving manner and to keep his immune system healthy and filled with protective energy. This meant cancer cells would have a much harder time taking hold and proliferating. We checked in regularly to make sure he was still clear, and Ben became increasingly confident in his sensing abilities as time passed.

Specific Suggestions

Feeling the Presence of Life Energy in Your Body was the first step for Ben. Remember your entry point may differ. The following suggestions are especially helpful to those who were neglected as children or who experienced physical trauma, which left them with reduced bodily sensation due to frozen, numb, or painful places. These are places of severe disruption in your body presence. If you have a hard time feeling your body's internal landscape — your insides — for any reason, the suggestions that follow may be helpful.

Set aside time to practice with Explorations 1 and 2 regularly; daily would be optimal. While using Exploration 1, if sensations elude you, try these strategies.

1. Compare density, weight, and color qualities in different areas of your body. For instance, you could ask yourself:
    a) Does my chest area feel lighter or darker than my belly?
    b) Does my head feel heavier or lighter than my chest?
    c) Which feels denser, my right or my left leg?
    d) Does my spine feel fuller or emptier than the rest of my torso?

2. Ask yourself about different qualities in a specific area. For example, If my heart felt like a color, would it be orange-red or blue-green or brown-red or some other color?

3. When you ask yourself one of these questions, allow the answer to pop in quickly. Listen to your first hit. Whatever comes is right. Do not edit or judge your answer. Just let it drop into your conscious awareness and acknowledge it. Only you know your answers; you just didn't know you knew them until now.

4. Take time now to record your sensations by writing in a journal, drawing, or painting. A few minutes of recording this way can bring these subtle sensations to a more concrete level.

5. When you find that you are feeling more sensations with Exploration 1, without all the extra questions, you can let go of these extra steps and move on to Exploration 2, Grounding and Filling. It will be easier to identify nourishing, nurturing sensations for yourself, as you sharpen your inner awareness skills. Important sensation clues will also drop naturally into your conscious awareness, as they did for Ben, the more you work with Exploration 2.

Parenting My Volatile Child

Melinda is the mother of Justin, a sweet but volatile child with mild autism. Justin has difficulties processing through his sensory system, so he constantly feels bombarded with smells, sounds, and visual stimuli in his world. He alternately withdraws completely into his own world or engages in loud temper tantrums, which leave Melinda exhausted and overwhelmed.

When I first met Melinda, she was sitting with her legs tucked up under her, lotus-style, in one of my classes. As we began, I asked everyone to place both feet on the floor to start grounding and filling. She looked surprised, but complied immediately. However, the first chance she got, she tucked her legs under again. Later, when people began to share their experiences, a woman next to Melinda welled up with tears. Although she was polite, I could tell Melinda was agitated by the emotion being expressed. In fact, I could sense her getting more uncomfortable with each passing moment. I gently asked her to put her feet back on the floor and to ground one more time into the earth's energy field.

Melinda later shared with me her experience in that moment:

Suddenly, I was remembering when I was a child and my parents argued viciously with each other. Once when I was about eight years old, watching TV in the family room, my parents got into a huge argument in front of me. I wanted to curl up and disappear, and energetically that's just what I did — curled up and disappeared, so that they would not notice me and yell at me. My brother got the bulk of their attention because he fought back, and he fared far worse than I did. So my defense strategy worked really well for me then, but it wasn't working in the class. And I suddenly realized it doesn't work with my son. He needs me to stay steady, calm, and present — not disappear.

I've been shrinking away and disappearing from volatility for years. It has been exhausting to survive that way. And there I was doing it in class. When I allowed myself to expand downward, I felt nurturing sensation in my legs and feet for the first time in a long time. It felt weird at first and a little scary, but I did it anyway and very quickly felt better.

Melinda visibly relaxed when she was able to feel her feet and legs in a good way again. She was reclaiming her Full Body Presence. I could sense that she felt steadier and safer. Her face softened. Her shoulders dropped. Her spine rested back against her chair. The emotional sharing in the room no longer bothered her. In fact, she reported feeling more connected to the other people in the room without feeling agitated or ungrounded.

If Melinda were an object instead of a person, I would say that the flow of life's energy, like electricity, now has a ground, a connection that makes it more manageable and less scary. She is no longer about to be "fried" by the emotional charge in a room or by her old, emotionally charged memories.

Weeks after the classroom incident, Melinda shared this with me:

The interesting thing is, now that I am living more in my legs and feet, feeling the earth under me, I can stay therapeutically present with my son, and he is much calmer. He is having fewer emotional swings. I hadn't realized it before, but it's as though his emotional mood swings and volatility were his way of responding, in the only way he knew how, to my lack of Full Body Presence.

When we talked even later, she shared this:

As a longtime practitioner of yoga and meditation, I had cultivated a clear sense of how to calm my nervous system using my yoga breathing and meditation. However, I couldn't sustain it for very long outside my meditation room. I could be calm while still and alone but not in the fray of my life as the mother of a special-needs child. Since the class and work with the Explorations, I have been practicing putting my feet on the floor and connecting and filling up as often as I can during my day, and I have noticed that I am consistently more able to walk in my world and feel that sense of being full and steady.

People's opinions don't sway me the way they used to. I can tolerate and even enjoy certain situations in my life that I could not before. I can now have a flow of nourishing energy all the way through my body, not just from the base of my spine on up through my torso. And as I establish a full container, my presence gets bigger and life feels easier.

Looking back, I realize that my old shrinking habit cut off the flow of earth energy to my legs and feet. And when I shrank, anyone's emotional process around me felt overwhelming. Once I learned how to reconnect, I felt more of my internal landscape. I could be in new situations and enjoy them — even learn from them. As the mother of a special-needs child with lots of emotional ups and downs, these abilities are having a huge impact.

Also, my resilience is better. I know when to slow down and rest, and I can go for longer periods of time without resting. I have more stamina. Somehow, having a nice strong sense of my feet and legs connected to the ground under me gives me the support I have never had before.

Melinda's son did not miraculously become a model child because of her newfound steadiness, but Justin did become significantly calmer. When things did upset him, because Melinda could feel her body and remain fully present, she could hold a therapeutic presence and choose healthier resources. She was more able to respond in ways that were helpful and useful to Justin and everyone else. She also began standing her ground and speaking up for herself with the rest of the family. Initially, this caused waves, but as she stayed steady and connected to the needs of everyone (including herself), things slowly became smoother and happier.

Six months later, Melinda shared more:

I am astonished at how much closer I feel to my son and husband these days. We actually have times that I can call fun — even joyful — sweet moments of connection that I have never felt before. I am realizing I had been living my life at a functional level, but still constantly on red alert, waiting for Justin's volatility to erupt. So, I was never really able to relax. Reclaiming my connection to the earth through my feet and legs was pivotal for me. Once I had a sense of the ground under me on a consistent basis, I just felt steadier and more relaxed. When I go back and remember those years as a kid, all curled up and small, I know that person was me, but it doesn't have to be me for the rest of my life! I am back in school now, getting my master's degree, following through on a lifelong dream. I am moving forward in my world, not disappearing. It feels so much better.

Specific Suggestions

Feeling the Presence of Life Energy in Your Body was the first step for Melinda. If you are someone who has not been in the lower half of your body much, or if you do not feel a friendly, easy connection with the earth's energy field, you may find the following suggestions valuable. They also apply to anyone who tends to live in their head or has a tendency to contract under stress, pulling in tightly or pulling up and out of the body.

These suggestions may also be valuable for someone who has years of experience doing yoga and meditating in the seated lotus position. In yoga, I was taught to concentrate on bringing energy from the base of my spine up and out the crown, or to circulate the life force in my torso. In doing so, I was totally bypassing my legs and feet and their connection to the earth. I had a strong presence when I was meditating but not when I was walking in my world. If this sounds familiar, give these suggestions a try.

1. Start with Exploration 1 to ascertain where you are comfortable and present in your body and where you are not. Be curious, not judgmental.

2. Practice Exploration 2 to connect and fill up. Then work with Exploration 3 to lovingly hold and eventually reclaim the parts of yourself you are locked out of or do not inhabit for some reason. Please be sure that your feet are in contact with the earth when you do this.

3. Usually, as you move back into the parts of yourself that you vacated, the reason for the disruption in your presence will show up in some form. It may take the form of a spontaneous memory, such as Melinda had, or perhaps a dream, later

recalled, that tells the story. I encourage you to journal when you identify a disruption; sometimes the root of the disruption emerges when journaling in a stream of consciousness manner after the Exploration.

4. Commit to working with all three Explorations on a regular basis until all the layers of the old pattern have been released. This will give you a much steadier sense of the totality of yourself, so that you can walk in the world with your power and Full Body Presence.

Burned Out from Caring for My Elderly Mom

Sandra is the primary caregiver for her elderly mother, Edna. She moved back in with her mother three years ago to care for her after her mother's stroke. Edna has been difficult to handle because of her own lifelong fearfulness in addition to her physical neediness after the stroke. She insists that Sandra do everything for her and won't allow anyone else to come in to cook or clean. Sandra's life has been sorely curtailed, as she has tried to take good care of her mom.

Sandra and I began by doing Exploration 1, Opening Awareness. She dissolved into tears of frustration as she realized how empty she felt. Her spine was tight. Her heart felt like a closed fist. Her bones felt empty to her. She really was at rock bottom on many levels, and from this place, her mom's fear was running both their lives. Sandra was no longer clear about what she herself needed.

We went immediately on to Exploration 2, Grounding and Filling, taking time to fill every nook and cranny of her system. When we completed that Exploration, Sandra's bones felt much juicier, and she had a small cushion of energy with which to work. Her tears stopped, and she was feeling steadier. However, Sandra's heart still felt closed to her. So we proceeded to Exploration 3, in which her heart could be held by loving, unconditional energy. When Sandra held her heart, a younger version of her emerged, and the tears began again: "I just want to please her. I have tried so hard all my life to please her, and nothing is ever good enough. No matter how much I do, she is still critical. I just want her to love and appreciate me."

As waves of tears washed through her, Sandra slowly relaxed. Her heart was softening, and her face was more open. She had reclaimed a part of herself. When the tears stopped, I asked how her heart felt.

"The fist is looser now, but I need to get it open all the way. It still hurts — less now, but it still hurts."

I asked her to notice how her backbone felt behind her heart. As she tuned in to her spine, I sensed her chest expanding bit by bit. Then I asked her to feel her sitting bones on the chair. She relaxed even more. I asked her to notice her feet making contact with the earth again. I could sense her system steadying out.

I asked Sandra what her younger self would like to say to the Sandra of today. "My younger self is no longer crying," she said. "She just needs to be held. The adult in me knows that my mother is like a wounded kid who never grew up. But my younger self still wanted her to mother me the way a mother should — to love me unconditionally, support me, and tell me I am wonderful. I never got that."

This realization expanded Sandra's perceptual lens as she held the possibility of experiencing her mother more accurately. She was silent for a few minutes.

"She is not capable of giving me that, is she?"

I concurred. Sandra looked sadder, but somehow more at peace. I asked what her younger self wanted to be doing if she didn't have to worry about pleasing her mother. She was silent again, but a smile was growing on Sandra's face as her perceptual lens expanded even more.

Then she said, "I would want to go dancing again with my friends — like I used to do. I would want to go watch the sunset on the beach. I would call my college roommates and go to dinner. I would take an entire afternoon to read a favorite novel and listen to my favorite music."

Sandra was on a roll; I let her keep going as her Full Body Presence

returned. We brainstormed about how to get competent help to stay
with her mom so she could get time away. At first, she was not as sure
about this aspect of the plan, but she practiced being grounded and full
as she planned how she would speak with her mom about getting help.
Sandra was steady and clear when she left the session.

One week later, she was back. She listened to Exploration 2, Grounding and Filling, every day and also just before she talked with her mom
— so that she could go into the interchange with Full Body Presence.
Her mom went into her habitual fearful, clingy response when Sandra
announced that she had arranged for a highly recommended nurse to
take her place the following week for several hours every day. Sandra
described the interchange:

> I was pleasantly surprised by how steady I felt. I could clearly see
> her for the scared little girl that she is inside, instead of the tyranni-
> cal boss I have let her be all these years. As I continued to hold a
> therapeutic presence and she saw that I was not backing down, Mom
> quieted down. We were able to talk about it in a civil way. She did get
> manipulative again the next morning. But I stayed grounded, and
> she eventually backed down that time as well. By the third time, when
> she started her old routine the following day, I was firmly in my Full
> Body Presence, and it hardly lasted any time at all. I know she is still
> afraid, but she seems less so as I stay steady and clear about my de-
> cisions. I think that throughout the years, I have been joining her in
> her fear. Now she seems to be joining me in my steadiness. It is great!

I shared with Sandra that when you put several working pendu-
lums in a room together, they all eventually come into synchrony with
the largest one. In other words, the largest energy presence in the room
prevails. I encouraged her to continue to be the largest presence in the
room whenever she is with her mother. Sandra was pleasantly surprised
to find that when she changed the energy dynamic in their relationship,
everything else shifted with it.

Life is getting more interesting every week for Sandra. She is practicing holding her ground and being the largest presence in the room

repeatedly as her mom tries unsuccessfully to get back the control in their relationship. Sandra is taking more time for herself, getting her life back day by day. She is naturally bringing her Full Body Presence into other areas of her life as well, and so she is enjoying everything in her life more. The principle of Feeling the Presence of Life Energy in Your Body has given Sandra back her life. Her perceptual lens has also expanded, and she is choosing resources moment to moment that maintain her Full Body Presence.

Specific Suggestions

Feeling the Presence of Life Energy in Your Body was Sandra's first step. If you are exhausted from caring for an aging or ill family member, or if you find yourself subject to manipulation by others, the following suggestions will be valuable for you.

1. Regular (daily if possible) practice of Exploration 2 is key. You want to get to a point where it is a habit to be living your life from a full container. Your wisest decisions are made when your container is full and connected to healthy resources.

2. Use Exploration 3 to discover where you are losing energy. Find the limiting belief you are losing energy to and work to resolve it. Exploration 3, segment 2, can help you with this. Sandra was losing energy to the younger version of herself that desperately wanted her mom's approval; this child-self was basically operating from the limiting belief that she was not worth taking care of. Sandra had to release that belief and step back into her power to resolve this.

3. Tune in to your inner wisdom, and ask what you need to be doing in your life to rejuvenate and care for yourself. What nurturing, nourishing self-care do you need? Commit to caring for yourself every day. And then do it!

4. Keep track of when you start to contract or feel an energetic disruption in your body. Commit to practices that help you to

be the largest presence in the caregiving relationship so that you can take care of yourself as well.

Feeling the Presence of Life Energy in Your Body is an essential element in healing and connecting with your inner wisdom, which is a vital component of your navigational system. Ben's ability to feel his abdomen, Melinda's ability to feel her legs and feet, and Sandra's ability to feel more energy in her heart were the necessary first steps for transforming their lives. From this point, all the other principles of choosing, trusting, integrating, and expanding easily follow.

Ben, Melinda, and Sandra derived different benefits from the principle of feeling. Ben gained a clear sense of his internal landscape and inner wisdom that saved his life. Melinda gained a sense of belonging through her feet and legs, which led to a greater sense of belonging in her Full Body Presence with her family and the world. Sandra regained her vitality and joy as she learned how to feel her Full Body Presence and create a life separate from her mother's fear. All discovered how much easier and more natural life is when it is experienced from inside their bodies.

PRINCIPLE 3
INTEGRATE Life Energy Throughout Your Entire System.

Integrating a felt sense of nurturing life energy throughout your entire body helps you establish a full personal container with strong, flexible, healthy boundaries.

The following two stories show how the principle of Integrating Life Energy Throughout Your Entire System can be the entryway for beginning the healing and transformation process. Other principles are also included in these stories, but integrating opened the door in both these cases.

I'm Not Afraid of Hard Work

Julie is a sharp, intelligent woman, who works in corporate management. Her discipline and focus enable Julie to really make things happen. She has mastered getting the job done. Julie grew up on a farm, where she learned about hard work. In fact, working hard is her primary default stance in life. Ask Julie to do something or learn something, and she will immediately jump in and work very hard to succeed. With straight-ahead focus and an eye on the goal, she has spent most of her life pulled forward, anticipating the next moment.

In the course of a bodywork session with me, Julie was trying to slow down and let her awareness and her presence spread out so that she could feel more relaxed. At one point, she was trying to bring her energetic awareness, her presence, into a place in her gut where she could not feel much energy. She chuckled and said, "There I go again, working hard at relaxing and spreading out!" Julie realized her work was actually to back off, let go of the goal, and let her softening awareness just be there, without trying to do anything.

As my hands were cradling her gut, I recognized that "not afraid of hard work" was a default stance for me as well. Throughout my life, I have constantly brought this default stance to my conscious attention and made a decision to relax and let go. I know that I am not alone in this. Among the thousands of students I have taught, I would say that many people operate out of this default stance. The expression "If you want to get something done, give it to a busy person" originated somewhere!

The invisible mandate to work hard can give us a sense of completion and competence, but it doesn't do much for our ability to simply be present in each moment. I am stuck in a doing mode when I am living from this default stance, and when this is the case, it is hard to enjoy my life. It is hard to be anywhere but in the future when I am working hard. I think about how much I am getting done, about how happy I'll be when I finish, how accomplished I will feel, how others will be happy with what I have accomplished.

So, how could I facilitate Julie's healing and perhaps my own? First, I committed to holding a space for her that held no judgment and was kind and loving. We laughed together, and I let my hands on her gut get even softer and more present, melding with her. I committed to simply being a Full Body Presence for her, which would allow her to do the same for herself. To do this, I knew I had to be as clear and present in myself as I could in that moment.

I could not be secretly judging myself. I could not be working hard to make Julie relax. I could not have an agenda for her. I needed to simply be present with her as she learned from herself and my therapeutic presence how to relax and let go of the goal. I had to relax in order to help her learn to relax. I found this fun. We both started giggling and then laughing and then really laughing at how we normally thought we needed to focus so hard in our work in order to survive and succeed. We were laughing so hard that our stomachs hurt. It felt really good.

When Julie and I were able to relax, we both felt as though our boundaries were more flexible and healthier — our containers more full and with an easy flow of nurturing life energy. The sharp focus that we were both so familiar with had softened, and we had opened to more joy and laughter. At the end of the session, Julie reported feeling more energetic awareness throughout her entire system. This had been a groundbreaking session for her. She had attained a sense of ease she had never experienced before. I felt full and happy too. This was one of those sessions where to give truly was to receive.

Specific Suggestions

Julie's first step was to integrate a sense of relaxation throughout her entire system. If you are the kind of person who works hard, has a difficult time relaxing, or spends a lot of time thinking about the future, the following suggestions may be valuable.

1. Exploration 2 is the key here. Filling up regularly and allowing yourself to meet your world in a full and relaxed manner is crucial to creating grace and ease in your life. For a better balance between work and rest, while you are grounding and filling, ask what you specifically need in order to slow down and rest. Observe how your cells and tissues respond to the questions about slowing down. One of my favorite questions in this category is to ask how my favorite massage therapist's hands would feel resting on my shoulders. If I feel my shoulders drop significantly with that question, I know I need to slow down and get a massage.

2. If you are trying to discern what would be best for slowing down, ask your inner wisdom questions that involve possible activities, such as a massage, a soak in a warm bath, time off with nothing in your schedule, slow dancing to your favorite music, petting your cat or dog, sharing a cup of coffee with a friend — you get the idea. See how you feel inside as you imagine yourself doing an activity. Then schedule something for yourself. If the activity that resonates for you isn't within practical range, soak it up through your mind's eye. And soak it up through all the other parts of you that know how to take in nurturing sensation. You can tell by your internal response what your next step should be.

3. Until I was in a relaxed, slower, healthier space, I could not conceive of a way to proceed in my life without the "work hard" default stance to drive me. But when I slowed down

enough to feel what daily rhythm actually nourished me, I could make better choices in my life. Some people have to crash and burn to figure out that overwork isn't healthy for them. I highly recommend the choose-to-slow-down-and-take-a-deeper-look approach. And frankly, once you are doing the grounding and filling in Exploration 2 on a daily basis, your inner wisdom will begin to speak to you about what pace is healthiest for you.

4. Take time off to engage in activities that are relaxing and energizing at the same time. From weekend and monthlong retreats to daily meditation and yoga classes or religious services that allow you to slow down and turn inward to reflect — these and other possibilities can be nourishing activities for people whose default stance is to work too hard. Life is too short to miss the good stuff that we can only receive when we have slowed down enough to take it in.

Teenage Daughter's Power Struggle

Mary and her fourteen-year-old daughter, Kelly, are constantly at odds. When Mary asks her daughter questions about her plans for the evening or her life in general, Kelly feels controlled and manipulated. Mary just wants to know that her daughter is safe and taking care of herself. Kelly pulls away and gets evasive in response to feeling controlled. Mary then worries that Kelly is hiding something, that she is doing something dangerous or stupid. This dynamic gets played out multiple times in any given week. Both were miserable when they arrived at my door.

When I explained to Kelly that our session would be about getting her power in relationship with her mother, she liked the idea, but I could tell she was still wary of me. Mary has known me for a number of years, so Kelly wasn't yet sure where my loyalties lay. I explained to Kelly that in our session I would give them both a set of skills to help them navigate their relationship into a win-win dynamic. Kelly was willing to give it a try.

First, I asked them to sit facing each other a comfortable distance apart. I asked them to close their eyes and took them through Exploration 1 to get a baseline sensation to work from. Afterward, Kelly said she felt "fine" and "normal." Mary was more discerning; she realized that her energy presence leans toward Kelly, taking up all the air space between them. Mary's energetic awareness was out in front of her, not integrated throughout her entire system. When Kelly heard what her mom shared, her face lit up and she responded, "I can feel that — like a pressure on my chest. Back off, Mom!"

Mary then worked to get her energy presence to return to her body to integrate throughout her system. After some instruction on grounding and filling, Mary's presence returned to her own body. Kelly was visibly more relaxed. When I asked Kelly how she was feeling, she reported, "I cannot believe how much better I feel!"

I then asked Kelly to check in and see where the majority of her energy presence is located. "It's odd," she replied after some quiet. "My mom was in front of herself, but I feel more of myself in the back of my body and behind me, like I am hiding out a little bit." I affirmed that her presence was pulled back, probably trying to get space from her mom.

I asked Kelly if she would like to integrate her energetic awareness throughout her entire system by bringing her presence forward. I explained that if she wanted to be in her power with her mom, she had to fully inhabit her own body, not hang out somewhere behind it. Because she looked puzzled, I asked Kelly awareness questions to help her energy field, her presence, come forward. "Can you feel the rise and fall of your chest as you breathe?" I asked. "Does your belly move when you breathe?" Kelly had to move into those parts of her body to answer my questions. As she brought her energy presence more fully into herself, her mom silently but visibly relaxed.

"Now, Kelly, let your awareness expand out a little farther and tell me how your mom's presence feels to you now." After a bit of silence, a smile appeared on her face. Kelly opened her eyes to tell me.

"When we began, I hated my mom's presence. It was too much. It was pushing on me all the time. All I could think about was how to get away from her. Now, somehow, it doesn't feel that way. I am not sure how it does feel yet, but I don't hate it anymore."

I asked her how powerful she felt now compared to when we began. Kelly's wonderful grin appeared again.

"I do feel more powerful. Weird — how did you do that?"

I reviewed what she had done for herself — awareness returning to the front of her body, grounding and filling, and willingness to learn something new. I had just facilitated her in establishing Full Body Presence. The process had become easy and transparent for her, so she could repeat it at will.

When I returned to Kelly's mom to see how she was doing, she was a little worried. She understood that what she was doing was wrong but wondered how to connect in a way that would not make Kelly withdraw. Mary's energy presence had a focused intensity where her daughter was concerned. And although she now knew she could withdraw that intensity at will, there was a fundamental shift she needed to make in the quality of her energy presence in order for her relationship with Kelly to become a win-win one. Mary and Kelly needed a healthy connection, not abdication of power on Mary's part.

I needed Kelly's feedback on this next step to give it validity. So I asked her to relax fully into her body and give us feedback while Mary took the next step. I asked Mary to remember a time when she was happy and relaxed. She didn't share what she was thinking, but her whole face relaxed, her shoulders dropped, and a smile came to her face. I asked her to notice how she felt in her body at that moment. She described feeling soft and warm. Her intensity had dispersed. Kelly's face lit up, and she let her mom know how much safer it felt to be with her when she was like that.

I asked Mary to notice what had changed in her body. She said it was as though the molecules had spread out. She felt full, but more diffuse. With her container full, her boundaries felt clearer, yet softer and more flexible. The intensity was gone, and it felt peaceful.

When I asked her to notice how connected she felt to Kelly, she replied, "I feel more connected than before. How could that be?"

I explained that a softer, more diffuse energy presence is easier to connect with and feels safer. But it also requires that Mary stay grounded and full and that she keep her energy integrated throughout her entire system. When she opened her eyes, she maintained her state of Full Body Presence by drinking in her daughter, rather than moving out energetically to meet her. It felt wonderful to Kelly.

But we were not done. Relationship dynamics are not just made of energy presence, or its absence, but also of how we communicate verbally. I knew this part of their relationship had been rocky. I asked Kelly, "In the past, your mom's presence was too intense when she asked you questions about your life and friends, right?"

"I feel like she is trying to control me," Kelly blurted out.

Mary looked surprised. That was not her intention. I asked Mary what her intention is when she questions Kelly.

"I really just want enough information to know that Kelly is safe," Mary explained. "I do want her to learn to stand on her own two feet. I do not want to control her and keep her from learning that."

Now it was Kelly's turn to look surprised.

I asked Mary, "What information would help you to know that Kelly is safe?"

Mary made a short list of her requirements: needing to know the people Kelly is with, where they are going, whose parent will be present, and what time she will be home.

"So you aren't going to pry into the details of my social life? Ask me about who likes who, or exactly how the evening went, or anything else?" Kelly asked her mother.

"As long as you aren't doing things that are harmful to you, like drugs or drinking," Mary answered, "I trust that you will make good decisions with your friends."

Now Kelly was really surprised. "You'll trust me?"

"As long as I have enough information to be able to reach you quickly in an emergency or if you need help, I will trust you to begin to make your own choices."

I turned to Kelly: "Kelly, in order for your mom to have the information that will help her to know you are safe, you need to stay in your power and offer it to her, so she doesn't have to go into mom-interrogation mode."

Kelly promised she would try.

This was going to be a stretch for both of them, and they knew it. Kelly had to stay in her Full Body Presence to feel her power and interact with her mom from a more integrated place, instead of pulling away and reacting negatively or disrespectfully. Mary had to hold up her end of the bargain by not letting her presence go back to being too intense and invasive. She needed to ask her questions in a clear and grounded way, and let Kelly answer them. I agreed to help Mary ask appropriate questions.

When we finished, they were cautiously optimistic. In the weeks and months that have followed our session, Mary has checked back in daily with Exploration 2 and several times with Exploration 3 for support. She is learning to feel more throughout her body. She holds the fear in her heart in a loving, unconditional way and is learning to discern when she truly needs to be worried and when she can let it go. She called last week to tell me that she had discovered that her gut feelings are a lot more accurate about Kelly's honesty and safety than the fear and worry in her head. She is also exploring how to hold healthy boundaries around what she allows her daughter to do — how to be connected to her and yet support her healthy independence.

Their relationship is doing much better. It isn't perfect, but now they have the skills to correct their course when they start to veer off. When Kelly can stay in her Full Body Presence, which enables her to stand in her power, Kelly's interactions with her mom are much more productive and respectful. Naturally, there have been setbacks. Kelly has made mistakes, like all teenagers. When things go awry they can return to a healthier state more quickly, often within minutes or hours. Now they are able to sit together, check in with how present they are, and communicate from a more grounded, steady place.

Specific Suggestions

If you want to work with relationship issues, particularly complex or long-standing ones that may have multiple layers, the third segment of Exploration 3 can help. The following suggestions may also be valuable:

1. To discover what your energy presence is like in a particular relationship, listen to Exploration 1 as you bring that person to mind, as though they are sitting right across from you.

2. Notice where in your body you have sensation and where you have numbness. Notice if you are withdrawing or leaning into the other person energetically. Does any part of you open up or close off when you imagine being in this person's presence. For instance, when we fall in love, we tend to feel a sense of opening up in the presence of our beloved. When we are struggling in a relationship, we often feel parts of ourselves wanting to close up or protect us in the presence of the other person.

3. Use Explorations 2 and 3 to ground, fill up, and cradle with unconditional love the parts of yourself that feel locked out or not present in — those places where you experience a Disrupted Body Presence. Allow your energy field to expand into those areas and challenge any limiting beliefs you may have about living in those parts of your body.

If you are a teenager, you may feel as though you have to re-treat from or fight with your parents. Try being solidly grounded with Full Body Presence, as you negotiate what works for all of you. And if you are a parent, when you are grounded in Full Body Presence around your teenager, it is easier to feel what is right and what is off in any given moment. Trust your gut on this. Don't insist that your children be like everyone else, but also don't relinquish your power to them when something feels "off." It is your responsibility to guide your children safely through their teenage years. Don't walk away energetically in order to keep the peace. Doing so may create temporary har-mony, but you'll pay for it in the long run. Meet your children where they are, and call on them to be responsible human beings. Don't expect them to be perfect, and don't let them off the hook when they need to take responsibility for their actions. This is most easily accomplished when you are grounded and as full as you can be and working through your own issues so they don't get projected onto your children. Life is too short — enjoy it!

Integrating Life Energy Throughout Your Entire System is an essential element in establishing a full container from which to live and create using your unique gifts, whatever they may be. The principle of inte-gration is also essential in establishing healthy boundaries. It both gives you a sense of safety when you interact with others and strengthens your therapeutic presence, making you feel safe and healing to others.

With Julie's fuller, softer container, she experienced a lot more ease and joy — in my treatment room and in her day-to-day life — and her gifts flowed more effortlessly as she worked with others. When Kelly learned to integrate her energetic presence fully throughout her body, she was able to show up in her power and resolve issues with her mother instead of fighting about them. And when Mary's energy filled out, softened, and was integrated throughout her entire system, her daughter felt safe again in her presence. Then both could interact with minimal strife. Choosing to integrate was the initial and primary action that led to transformation in these lives. After integration, all the other principles easily followed.

Each of these three people derived different benefits from this principle. Julie gained a clear sense of ease, Kelly gained her power and a better ability to navigate because of that integrated power, and Mary gained a deeper sense of connection with her daughter at this critical point in Kelly's development. They all discovered how much easier and natural life feels when it is experienced from inside the body.

PRINCIPLE 4
EXPAND Your Perceptual Lens

Expanding your perceptual lens enables you to see clearly, release expectations and limiting beliefs, and open fully to life.

The next three stories illustrate the principle of Expanding Your Perceptual Lens as an entry into the healing and integration process. Other principles are included in these stories, but expanding opened the door in these three cases.

Critical Me

Heather called me for a session when she was three months out of recovery from a knee surgery that had left her sedentary for quite a while during the healing process. During that time, she gained back much of the weight she had lost in the last three years, and she felt overwhelmed by the thought of going back to the gym for her regular workout. Heather felt heavy and out of control where her body was concerned.

She was convinced she had gotten fat and that she was being lazy. Her normal Full Body Presence was disrupted on many levels.

After we took enough time to get grounded and full using Exploration 2, I checked in with Heather to see how she was currently feeling inside. She told me she felt sluggish and nauseous. In the next breath, she was muttering about her laziness. I asked her to remember how she had felt when she weighed less and was in better shape. She couldn't recall what that felt like at all. She couldn't get past her current feeling of sluggishness and the self-judgment that she was at fault. It had not yet occurred to Heather that there could be something else going on in her system, which was causing the sluggishness.

Having worked with Heather before, I recognized a familiar pattern, which was the limiting belief that if something was going wrong in her world, she was somehow always at fault. It had to do with her believing she was "not being good enough." Her perceptual lens was definitely narrow and cloudy.

In previous sessions, we had visited and revisited this particular limiting belief in many areas of her life. Heather had uncovered how her mother's critical attitude toward her as a child had seeded this belief. In past sessions, Heather had expanded her perceptual lens and realized this wasn't true, that she was in fact good enough. She was indeed an amazing and accomplished woman.

Heather had already healed this limiting belief in other areas of her being, so when we discovered the not-good-enough belief hanging out in the area of her body image, she had very little resistance to expanding her perceptual lens. Heather easily opened to the possibility that there was nothing inherently wrong with how she looked and that she was not at fault for feeling so low on energy. As she held that possibility, the tension from all her self-judgment began to melt. She felt more open and lighter. From there, she was able to take true responsibility for her health by asking herself what was wrong in her biology, in her body, if it wasn't about "being fat and lazy."

Expanding Heather's perceptual lens released a cascade of questions and curiosity — not judgment — about blood sugar, blood pressure, cholesterol, and hormone and thyroid functions. We had a detailed conversation with her body. Heather took notes as we went, so that she could take them with her to her next doctor's appointment. She had been dreading her next visit because of the weight gain and not yet returning to exercise. But that changed when she became a detective in pursuit of her own health. Heather actually began to look forward to solving this mystery with her physician.

We established that when she thought about returning to her full workout at the gym, it made Heather shudder. When we began to discuss the movement that her body could tolerate, Heather got an image of walking. I suggested she try an easy walk of twenty to thirty minutes a day for a couple of weeks. But Heather immediately hit another limiting belief: If she wasn't going full out, it wasn't good enough. A walk of twenty-five minutes a day at a comfortable pace wouldn't do it. Heather was raised with a relentless philosophy: "Make it count or don't do it at all. Work hard at everything you do. If it's worth doing, it's worth doing well." As a result, the only things she judged worthwhile were those she worked hard at. Heather quickly realized this was a limiting belief and opened to the possibility that she could see this differently: walking daily felt entirely doable, unlike returning in full force to the gym.

I asked Heather to practice grounding and filling daily, using Exploration 2, and to ask her inner wisdom what was going on, now that she was open to hearing what her body had to tell her. She was not to judge herself, which shut down further communication. Heather was open, optimistic, and ready to explore when we finished.

Specific Suggestions

Expanding the Perceptual Lens was Heather's entry into further healing, and she had to do it multiple times throughout her session. If you are someone who has a strong inner critic or you second-guess yourself a lot, segment 2 in Exploration 3 will be helpful in releasing limiting beliefs.

When our inner critic or judge is driving our bus, you can be sure they are using false or outdated limiting beliefs to stay in control. Often these limiting beliefs are not even in our conscious awareness. We just know that we are paralyzed or plagued by a bad feeling about ourselves for some reason. Heather is actually over the weight limit that is healthy for her and that feels good to her; however, she is a lot better equipped to handle this when she feels okay about herself. Then she is empowered to make changes that are lasting. When Heather's inner critic is haranguing her, she feels helpless, not good enough, and paralyzed to do anything about it.

When working on inner critic issues, I suggest using each Exploration daily until the pattern is released and you can think clearly about the issues at hand without an emotional charge.

1. Exploration 1 will help you to discern where in your body the inner critic and its associated pain are stationed.
2. Exploration 2 enables you to create a strong, full container with which to meet the area of pain or judgment in a powerful loving manner.
3. Exploration 3 is key to releasing any limiting beliefs so that you can move on in your life with more of you on board.

This process is fairly straightforward, but it can take time and repeated effort as the layers of limiting beliefs peel away. An outside facilitator is often helpful here because a long-standing, narrowed perceptual lens can be so deeply embedded that it looks deceptively like the truth. Remember Heather's layers. Don't let it get you down or stop your process if yet another layer shows up once you release the one above it. Know that you are indeed making progress.

As far as I can tell, this process goes on throughout our lives. As you saw with Heather, it gets easier once you have effectively released a few significant layers. Years ago, when Heather was releasing the first few layers of that ingrained belief about not being good enough, it took several sessions and buckets of tears as she tenaciously worked to release that false belief about herself. Later, as you could see from the session presented here, Heather easily and rather quickly peeled away another layer. You can do the same thing with practice.

My Anger Is Back

When John called and asked if he could come see me, he admitted that he and his wife had gotten into an old argument and that he had verbally raged at her. On top of that, his back had gone into spasm afterward. The next day, as soon as John walked in, I could see that he was in severe pain. In the bodywork session that followed, I used dialoguing skills from CranioSacral therapy, as well as my hands and therapeutic presence to help him. As his perceptual lens expanded, John was able to meet his rage and pain in an unconditionally loving way, which was healing.

We began the session with my hands gently cradling John's lower back and heart, the areas where he felt most disconnected. I could feel the tension, like steel cords, running through the palm of my hand that was on his back. John told me how the health of his lower back had steadily deteriorated over the last seven years and how angry he felt about it. "I can't play with my kids. I can't work in my yard. I am afraid of every small sensation, afraid that my back is about to go into yet another excruciating spasm. All I did was take a simple bike ride the last time it went into spasm. I feel fragile, and I hate feeling fragile."

I felt the intensity of his dilemma as he described it. His back got tighter under my hand as he talked. He had a severe disruption in his Full Body Presence, and it was manifesting right under my hands. It was clear to me that John could not see a way out of this cycle of injury, diminished capacity, and despair. His narrow perceptual lens had blinded John to the inner resources that could assist him in healing. At that moment, he was unaware that such resources even existed. So, our first step was to expand his perceptual lens so that he could see a new possibility for himself. My role was to help him access his deeper wisdom and meet the parts of himself he had locked away.

As we began, he allowed his awareness to drop into his lower back, describing what he noticed. His breath slowed and deepened as he settled in there.

"What strikes you first?" I asked gently. "Don't edit anything or think it through for validity. Just say what hits you first."

"It feels like a huge log. A tree trunk without the roots or branches."

I concurred. His lower back felt immovable, large, and hard, not like normal, healthy back tissue. His heart, under my other hand, had an echo of hardness as well.

"How long has it been like this?" I asked gently.

I felt the hardness soften as he answered, "I don't know, but I suddenly feel a very deep sadness as I let myself connect with your hands." His perceptual lens was starting to expand.

Again, I concurred, because I was feeling the sadness as it left him. I saw a small boy in my mind's eye, and moments later, John said to me, "I feel about four years old." The hardness softened even more as he described a bleak world: feeling alone, riding in a car, feeling terrified by his father's rage and his mother's inability to protect him. I asked John how the little boy coped with all of that.

"I did what I watched my father do. I got angry and stayed angry all the time, to create a protective shield around myself." He added, "I excelled in school so that I knew a lot, but I kept my anger out in front of me all the time. I won all my debates. I could lacerate my enemies verbally."

When I asked John how that related to the tree trunk in his back, he was quiet for a few moments before replying, "In order to stay angry all the time, my system has to stay on red alert, and that little boy in my lower back is still on red alert."

I asked him if he needed to be on red alert any longer. John was quiet, and I felt his back start to soften. His perceptual lens was expanding even further as he chuckled; I felt several more layers of his back relax. John realized he had unnecessarily carried that hardened boy in his rigid lower back all these years.

When I asked John if there is anywhere else that little boy would rather be, he replied quickly, "He wants to be held in my heart."

I felt the rest of his back soften as the little boy — John's vulnerability — moved in his mind's eye to his heart. I also felt his heart soften and fill under my hand, as the little boy curled up there.

Then a strange sensation began. I felt a numb, pins-and-needles sensation coming through my hand at John's lower back. It went on for about four minutes, and then it passed, as though his back was letting go of the residual numbness and rigidity. At that point, John fully returned to his lower back, which was no longer in pain. It felt soft and relaxed, and his heart had a good flow of energy moving through it. John's anger no longer owned him. Having expanded his perceptual lens, he was able to utilize his energetic awareness to integrate his presence throughout his entire system.

John shared how exhausted he felt in the aftermath of holding on tightly for so long. His breath deepened, and he went into a quiet relaxed state as we finished the session. His Full Body Presence was palpable. His anger had dissolved.

I suggested that the next time John felt a twinge of sensation in his back, he greet it with curiosity rather than anger and frustration. He should ask the sensation what it was trying to tell him. John agreed to try to do that and seemed much more at peace when we closed.

This story shows how the skills taught in this book and audio are utilized during a bodywork session. John could have worked on his own by holding his lower back in his energy hands, but it may have taken him longer to achieve the integration we reached in our session together. When the part of yourself that you want to reintegrate involves a highly charged, long-standing issue, like John's anger, a vital resource is often another human being who is grounded and conveys a therapeutic presence. That therapeutic presence supports you in exploring a vulnerable, scary place, without becoming overwhelmed by it.

As the facilitator of his healing process, it was most important I stay grounded, with Full Body Presence, so that I could provide the cushion of energy John needed to move through his deep-rooted problem. Throughout the session I repeatedly checked in to make sure I was as present as I could be for the unfolding healing process.

Also, remember how John brought his own energetic awareness to his lower back? As a client, when you add your energetic awareness to the alchemy of your healing sessions, the outcome is exponentially greater. So, stay present when you receive a healing session and use the skills you have learned here to get more out of every treatment you receive.

Specific Suggestions

The first step for John was to expand his perceptual lens around the pain in his back, energetically moving from seeing himself as a victim of back pain to experiencing and releasing the sadness and anger associated with it. Your entry point may differ. If you are struggling to integrate strong emotions and sensations that tend to take over your life and cause your relationships with others to suffer, the following information will be helpful.

1. First, recognize and own the emotion you're experiencing rather than projecting it onto someone else. Often, when we have strong emotions that feel unacceptable to us, we feel bad about them deep inside ourselves. As a result, we justify why the emotions are there and why we have a right to dump them

on others. The first step then is to recognize and take responsibility for your own emotions.

2. Notice where the emotion anchors in your body. Where is the root of your anger or the core of your fear in your body?

3. Use Exploration 3 to hold this place and work with the pain, or whatever is under the emotion, until it is integrated. Remember with a long-standing emotional pattern such as the one John exhibited, you may need to work with layers. You will greatly benefit from a well-trained hands-on therapist who can provide a therapeutic presence for your recovery.

New Ways of Perceiving a Self-Centered Friend

Trish is a wonderful, vivacious, caring woman. She is also self-centered in that she often does not take into account the needs of others or many of her time commitments. Years ago, when we would pick her up to go to a party together, she would invariably be anywhere from twenty to forty-five minutes late. Those of us waiting for her would get frustrated, then angry, and then resigned to what we saw as her lack of thoughtfulness. Sometimes we left her. But it never changed, no matter how much we complained. Trish would just laugh nervously and brush it off, saying she was sorry and would be on time next time.

I resolved this issue with her by expanding my own perceptual lens. I had to recognize that her lateness was her issue, and that I had enough power and presence not to be at the mercy of it. I still love her as a friend, but I recognize that she has this issue, which has nothing to do with me. I no longer ride to events with her; I see her at the event, in her own time. If she misses the beginning, so be it — it's not my issue. I don't ask her to bring an appetizer to a shared meal; I ask her to bring one of her delicious desserts. Although she is usually not ready when I visit her at her home, we can still connect and talk at her house without her being ready.

I have expanded my perceptual lens to clearly see Trish as she is, not as I want her to be, which leaves me disappointed. I love her for who she is, for her loyalty as a friend, and for her caring heart. In recognizing her limitations, I don't expect her to act like someone she is not. I chose to expand my lens to see how she actually operates in the world so that I could realistically meet her and enjoy her company. I no longer cling to a narrow vision of her as rude or inconsiderate.

Notice that I am not talking about how to make my friend change; I widened my perceptual lens. We get into trouble with one another when we expect others to act as we would and then take it personally when they don't. Instead of viewing others with our expectations and judgments, we can expand our perceptual lens. Think about limiting beliefs you may have been raised with around such issues as lateness, affection, being polite versus telling the truth, etc. Notice what you assume about the other person when they don't act the way you expect them to. Can you expand your perceptual lens and include a world where being on time is different from the way you were raised? Can you include another person's reality and walk in their shoes? If you are the person who is chronically late, can you walk in the shoes of the person you are keeping waiting?

Exploration 3, segment 2, specifically addresses expanding our perceptual lens. If this is an issue for you, use this resource. Remember, you may have to use it repeatedly if it is a long-standing or deeply ingrained belief you'd like to release.

During the period of my life when I was the mother of two young children, I was chronically late. I am still more relaxed about time than my husband. Also, having lived in several cultures, experiencing how differently people in southern Europe or on an Indian reservation treat time, has given me a more expanded lens on time. It doesn't mean I enjoy being kept waiting. It does mean I don't lose my Full Body Presence. And I am energetically aware of how the waiting is affecting me versus unconsciously being depleted by it (which I would have been at one point in my life).

Specific Suggestions

If you have friends or colleagues who, like Trish, cannot see beyond themselves in certain areas of their lives, or if you have a self-centered family member, someone you put on a pedestal, or someone you have written off because of some unmet expectation, the following instructions may be valuable.

1. Make the choice to expand your perceptual lens. It is important to be able to see the person for who he or she actually is rather than who you want or expect him or her to be. This takes the charge out of the issue and helps you decide what to do about your unmet expectations in a more clearheaded manner.

2. To get beyond your disappointment, anger, or frustration, you may want to begin by asking yourself what you are expecting from someone that you are not getting. This expectation may be outside of your conscious awareness; however, if you sit with the question for a short while, it will often come to you. Sometimes someone close to you who has heard you complain about this person can help you with this.

3. Next, examine how you are interpreting someone's inability to do what you want or expect. Some of these situations may resonate:

    •   Someone who is consistently late for commitments
    •   Someone who misinterprets your requests and does something different than you had asked
    •   Someone who does not offer to help in a situation in which you would have offered to help
    •   Someone who remains silent when you think something should have been said or someone who speaks when you think silence is needed
    •   Someone who does not see you or your needs clearly, consistently attributing things to you that are not true

- Someone you think should be perfect because he or she knows so much more than you (How could they make a mistake?)

4. What do you decide about such a person and about yourself given this behavior? (This could range from judging someone as bad or inferior in some way to judging yourself as not good enough or unlovable.)

5. How could you see this differently? How else could you interpret the words or actions? Really stretch here to expand your perceptual lens on the person, event, or situation. What else could the actions mean? Imagine the opposite of what you originally thought; how would that story play? Can you be open to the possibility that the truth lies somewhere in between?

6. When you have expanded your lens sufficiently, often you start to see this person or situation more accurately — as they are — rather than what you judge them to be. You will know this is the case when you no longer feel the same old charge when you think of them. For instance, if I forget and ask Trish to bring the appetizer, and she shows up forty-five minutes late, I don't get angry with her. I am frustrated with the situation, but mostly, I am frustrated with myself for forgetting that this is who she is.

7. Utilize Exploration 3 through all three segments to clear the whole range of issues, from expanding your awareness to healing limiting beliefs and feeling deeper ease in your relationships.

Expanding Your Perceptual Lens is an essential element in healing and standing in your power, even in the face of conflicting external influences.

The inner screen of our navigational system is clearer and more accurate when our perceptual lens expands. This is also the principle that teaches us to gather new information when we need to resolve an issue in our lives. Finding a book, embracing a new point of view by listening to someone else's perspective, learning about other cultures and religions are all helpful ways to expand one's perceptual lens.

Heather's entire health issue shifted when she expanded her perceptual lens to see herself in a different light. John's physical healing could unfold once his perceptual lens on his back pain expanded. I maintained a connection with my friend when I expanded my perceptual lens to see her more accurately and released my limiting beliefs about time.

As you can see in these stories, once the door was opened, all the other principles of feeling, choosing, trusting, and integrating easily followed. Expanding our perceptual lens can initiate the establishment of Full Body Presence, where we can listen to our internal landscape and operate from our navigational system rather than from fears and limiting beliefs.

PRINCIPLE 5
CHOOSE Nourishing Resources Moment to Moment

*Choosing moment to moment to connect to healthy resources
requires commitment, courage, and kindness;
it provides you with a steady foundation
and a deep sense of inner peace.*

The next two stories illustrate how the principle of Choosing Nourishing Resources Moment to Moment can be an entry into healing and transformation. Other principles are involved in these stories, but choosing opened the door in these two cases.

Wise Choice for Third Marriage

Deborah is now in her early forties, happily married with three children. But this was not always the case. As a younger woman, Deborah married her first husband because she thought she should. All her friends were married, and her mother and grandmother had married by age twenty-one. Deborah thought it was what she was supposed to do. She made the choice from the "ought to" in her head rather than from her inner wisdom. She had no one to model making wise choices from a Full Body Presence, and without energetic awareness, she had no way of contacting her inner wisdom.

Within a few years it became obvious that her relationship was ending; they both wanted very different things. Deborah did not have the skills or the internal resources to resolve their differences. She divorced her husband and married again very quickly in order to remedy the mistake she felt she had made ending her previous marriage. No one in her family had ever divorced, and her shame felt overwhelming. To get away from it, she married a man she didn't really have feelings for but who looked like the kind of man she should marry. This relationship proved to be abusive, further disrupting Deborah's body presence. She sensed this somehow and left that marriage within a year.

With two marriages in ruins, Deborah finally stopped running from herself. She chose to begin nurturing herself by learning the skills taught in Exploration 1. As she learned to ground and fill, healing her Disrupted Body Presence, she strengthened her ability to discern healthier resources. Using Exploration 3, Deborah learned to gently meet and lovingly hold the pain in her heart and the shame in her belly. With time, they dissolved and healed. Deborah relaxed and gave herself permission to live by her inner timing, instead of rushing to do what others thought was correct. Her discernment was developing, so that Deborah reliably made better and better decisions for herself.

When Deborah met her current husband, she did not act too

quickly, as she had previously done. She made a strong commitment to let herself fully explore what she wanted. She felt a growing sense of strength and worthiness for the first time in her life, and her Full Body Presence developed. When she made the decision to remarry, it was with a clarity, steadiness, and sense of inner peace she had not had before.

Deborah now knows what she wants and practices asking for it in her relationship. She is willing to negotiate differences with her husband, and her current marriage is a healthy and fulfilling one. Deborah has a clear enough sense of herself internally to navigate through her relationship without losing her integrity. She has flourished creatively as well. Everyone is a winner in this equation — Deborah, her husband, their children, and her creativity. She continues to choose nourishing resources moment to moment and keeps her container full and her navigational system intact.

Specific Suggestions

Choosing Nourishing Resources Moment to Moment was the first step for Deborah. If you tend to make unhealthy choices based on fear, shame, or guilt or you make good choices most of the time but also find yourself racked with fear, shame, or guilt because you fear making the wrong decision, these suggestions might be helpful to you.

1. To move beyond fear, shame, or guilt, it is important to change our internal resonance. When we are dominated by fear, shame, or guilt, our system reverberates dissonantly with those emotions. We often feel this tension when we slow down and tune in. On the other hand, when we are energetically full and connected to healthy resources, our resonance is deep and harmonious. This resonance is the signature of Full Body Presence. It is a state of being that is life-giving. It has a hum or a vibration to it, which sustains us over time. This resonance is also a signal that we have a container that can hold and heal any fear,

shame, or guilt within us. The following steps will help you shift your resonance in a healthier direction.

2. Start with Exploration 2, Grounding and Filling, to establish a full container with which to operate. When we are not feeling full and present, it is easy for fear to sway our lives. When we are grounded with Full Body Presence, we can readily discern what we feel inspired to do versus what we are afraid may happen.

3. Once you have identified where the pain and disconnect are anchored in your body, utilize Exploration 3 to hold and unconditionally love this place. Do so until it resolves and integrates, so that you can love all of you.

4. Regular practice of all of the Explorations is important and leads to life choices that are informed by your inner wisdom. Know that emotions such as fear, shame, and guilt can be powerful, hidden instigators of repeated self-destructive behavior. Be kind and gentle with yourself, as you uncover and heal the places within you where difficult emotions are trapped. The payoff for healing these places is immense.

5. Finally, please work with the second and third segments of Exploration 3. They are designed to help you trace and heal any limiting beliefs entwined with fear, guilt, or shame, which compromise you and your relationships. Such healing will provide you with a steady foundation and a deeper sense of inner peace.

I Don't Know What I Want from My Husband

(NOTE TO READER: *If you are experiencing challenges in your most intimate relationship, carefully read this account. Following the story, specific suggestions are listed which can help those who suspect that they may be accommodating others instead of authentically showing up and getting their needs met as well. There is also a section with specific suggestions for healing relationships.*)

Jodi and Philip have been consciously working to improve their marriage for years. They are now at a pivotal point, one that appears for all couples somewhere in the journey of their relationship. It is the time when fundamental change must happen for one or both partners if the relationship is to continue to grow and flourish. What I have found is that the energy skills taught here immeasurably support and deepen that level of fundamental change, as well as related work such as individual or couple's therapy and other forms of bodywork and healing.

The following happened while Jodi and Philip were in my office for an appointment together. We usually talk first, and then they each take turns getting on the treatment table for a hands-on CranioSacral session, in which the other person helps out. The following account is from Jodi, who describes her half of the session as she moved from the threshold of her relationship with Philip into a deeper place. Jodi begins with the hard realizations she recently came to in a couple's therapy session.

> I recognized that I am a classic accommodator to everyone else's needs. I rarely know what I really want deep down. I say "yes" in far too many circumstances when I want to say "no." I give people what they want, so they'll leave me alone. I feel invisible in my life in many ways. I am realizing now that I really was invisible as a child. My alcoholic father never really saw me at all. He was too wrapped up in his own pain. My mother was an accommodator as well and ambivalent about having children, probably because of my dad's alcoholism. All three children felt her ambivalence at some level, but I especially did.
>
> I have recently become aware of how I overcompensate for that feeling of invisibility by being very funny or entertaining. I am excellent at sensing what is going on with others, but to the detriment of knowing myself.

Jodi is seeing herself accurately here. At times, her presence is scattered and hard to connect with. In certain moments when we are

together, we are absolutely in sync, but the next moment she is gone.
Jodi continues:

> I am just realizing that I have serious difficulty knowing what I re-
> ally want in my marriage. Philip wants to connect more deeply with
> me. He's done his own work of backing off and not judging and
> badgering me. And you know how I have worked to open up to him
> — so many years of therapy and bodywork to resolve my childhood
> traumas. Now the issue is really coming to a head in our marriage. I
> feel stuck. I can see what I am doing; I just don't know how to move
> through this. I don't know how to make healthy choices for myself.

The process of being in relationships that nourish everyone requires
courage, skill, and commitment — and it is well worth the work involved. In fact, the latest brain research shows that when love and compassion are present, the brain lights up and operates to its fullest
capacity. We truly are meant to live in a deep sense of interconnectedness, and our relationships are a huge part of that process.

Whether we are talking about a beloved mate, a child, a best friend,
a parent, a boss, or a colleague, the principles of a healthy relationship
all rest on the same foundation. This is the steady foundation that Full
Body Presence provides and that enables you to choose what is life-
giving and to say "no" to what is energy-draining. Within that knowing of yourself and your needs, there are many twists and turns on the
path to healthy and enjoyable relationships. All start, though, with full
presence.

Let's return to Jodi and Philip in my office. She just shared that in-
sightful awareness about her lifelong pattern of accommodating others.
She is relaxing on the treatment table. My hands are supporting her
spine. Philip asks her where she would like to have his hands — in other
words, what she wants from him in this session. She tells him, "Oh,
hold anywhere; it doesn't matter."

It strikes me in that moment that she does not know how to make
contact with her deep inner knowing to choose what she truly wants,

what would be life-enhancing for her. I also sense that she is not in her bones, the deep recesses of who she is. She is in the more superficial parts of her body but not its most intimate chambers. Jodi doesn't have her Full Body Presence, and this is reflected in her lack of energetic awareness and her response to Philip.

I ask her to notice what she feels or doesn't feel deep inside her body, in her bones. She is quiet for a moment. She admits she cannot feel that part of herself. Gently guiding her to drop her awareness back in her body, into the part in contact with the treatment table, I use my relaxed flat hand on her spine to help her orient around a warm, physical sensation. Continuing to help her drop in, I ask, "What does the table feel like where your spine is touching it?" and, "Can you feel the back of your head on the table?" and then, "What do your feet feel like in Philip's hands?" My questions are designed to help her feel more of her internal landscape.

I feel her slowly settling deeper into her body, and as she does so, she spontaneously comes out with what she really wants from Philip. "I would like your hands on my heels, Philip, not the tops of my feet. Yes, that feels much better. Thank you." And later in the session when Philip tries to move too soon for her, she speaks up immediately and says, "Please stay there longer. Your hands there feel wonderfully settling."

Previously she was not even registering what she wanted, what her deepest needs were. Now, she is choosing clearly and asking for what she wants, without even thinking about it. Jodi finally knows what she wants! So as the session unfolded, she began to feel not only more of her spine but also the whole back. She palpably felt more settled and grounded. Jodi and Philip are both very pleased as we finish up, when she is fully present in her body.

None of her superficial chatter and jokes were there to keep intimacy at a distance. Jodi and Philip nuzzle each other, and I can feel a distinct difference in the level of their connection from when we began.

Jodi is now much easier inside, more deeply at home. Her needs and desires are not a mystery because she can feel what she needs — and it is delicious!

On their next visit, when I ask Philip how it is to have Jodi knowing and choosing what she wants, he tells me he is delighted. Then he grins and adds, "Well, it can be momentarily rough. Now, I get called on something that isn't working for her, but honestly, I love it. I have a wife who is real. I know where she stands. I can trust her presence in our relationship much more now. I have always known she was in there somewhere; I just didn't know how to get her to come out!" Jodi's grin in response is genuine, straight from her heart and bones!

Specific Suggestions

If you suspect you are an accommodator, Choosing Nourishing Resources Moment to Moment is probably your prime challenge. You may find the following questions helpful.

1. Do I try to please and nurture everyone else before myself?
2. Do I sometimes, or often, have difficulty even knowing what I need, what would feed and nourish me?
3. Do I find myself running around out there in my world, with little time for rest?
4. Is my self-care, when I do it, last on the list behind my significant other, my children, my pet, and so on?
5. Do I have a limiting belief(s) that says taking care of myself is selfish?

The strength of those with an accommodator default stance is that they are often accurate readers of what is going on with their loved ones. They may have spent their lives cultivating the skill of listening to the needs of others. So they are often good at anticipating the needs of those they love. This, however, must be balanced by choosing to meet their own needs — knowing how to drop deep inside, listen to their inner landscape, and access their navigational system.

If you answered "yes" to three or more of the questions above or you know someone who has this similar pattern, you may find the following suggestions useful. If you are an accommodator, it is important that you learn to slow down and listen to your deep inner places.

1. Practice regularly (daily for a time) with Exploration 1, Opening Awareness, and Exploration 2, Grounding and Filling.

2. Journal your inner experiences, sensations, emotions, and especially any limiting beliefs that show up.

3. Notice what areas of your body you are not living in or that have pain or numbness when you ask yourself the questions about accommodating other people. Often the sensations will be in your bones. When you approach such an area, a limiting belief may well come up that tries to persuade you "it is not safe to rest within yourself" or that you "must be on red alert, vigilantly scanning the environment in order to know that you are okay." Your particular limiting beliefs and messages may be slightly different. Listen to yourself, but recognize what these limiting beliefs are trying to convince you of so that you can expand beyond them.

4. Make sure that you are grounded and full. Use Exploration 3 to help you lovingly hold this place you feel locked out of or that you don't yet fully inhabit. Hold it and love it, as completely as you can at this time.

5. Be gentle with this process. As you come to completion, notice in particular what you are feeling inside. Any increased clarity about your needs? What internal itch needs to be scratched? What yearning has bubbled up?

6. Repeat this Exploration as many times as needed to release and integrate all the layers.

Deepening Your Interpersonal Dynamics

Take a moment now to bring to mind a relationship in your life. Using the skills from Exploration 1, Opening Awareness, take an internal reading on where you are in this relationship. Receive whatever information your body may have for you. Be as open as is possible at this time.

Sometimes our bodies give us messages that we don't want to hear, so we push them away. Do you sense any level of shielding yourself from this person? Many years ago, I was with my intimate other and discovered that when I stood across from him, I had a very subtle sense of shielding my heart from him. In my normal waking state of consciousness, I would never have said I felt that way about him, but as I stood there, my heart informed me that there were trust issues I needed to address.

Notice whether any limiting beliefs or painful phrases surface in your consciousness as you open to whatever awareness is there for you regarding this relationship. Is what appears familiar or a surprise? Is there a memory attached to your experience? If so, where do you feel it in your body?

The next step is to work with the skills from Exploration 2. Take time to get grounded and full. If the relationship you are exploring right now is a life-giving one, you will feel better and better as you fill up, and you will have more of yourself to share with this other person. The other person will probably experience you as more present, more available, and more joyful in the relationship. These skills are fabulous relationship enhancers, creating the optimal circumstances for ecstatic spiritual experience and deep intimacy. The simplest of interactions can become rich and delicious. Sometimes when I am feeling fully present, a heartfelt smile from someone I don't even know can warm me to my bones.

What about when we are emotionally hooked by what is going on in a relationship and feel tension, contraction, pain, numbness, fear, or shame in the presence of this other person? Although this is the richest area of learning for us as human beings, it is the hardest to want to work on. In successfully traversing and healing this kind of dynamic, we can grow immensely, opening up whole new worlds of opportunity. So how do we do this?

The three segments of Exploration 3 are designed to work together to lead you through the healing of layers of pain and disconnection. Healing happens in your own time, in a way you can integrate. Sometimes healing comes quickly in a rush of energy. Other times, it slowly moves in, until one day you realize you are not struggling anymore. Healing might be the realization that you need to change the nature of a relationship, for example, creating distance from someone who refuses to interact respectfully or delineating the boundaries with someone who has trouble with them.

Choosing Nourishing Resources Moment to Moment was an important first step for both Deborah and Jodi. When Deborah chose to slow down and explore her internal landscape, she was able to integrate energy throughout her entire system and establish Full Body Presence. This gave her a sense of steadiness and inner peace, which enabled her to make healthy choices on a moment-to-moment basis. Jodi made a commitment to connect more deeply with her internal landscape, and it gave her the courage to reclaim deep parts of herself. Then she was able to recognize and choose what she needed and wanted in a given moment. Jodi and Philip's choice to commit more deeply to their relationship exemplified the patience and kindness necessary for healing. Choosing healthy resources is an essential component for experiencing Full Body Presence.

I hope you have found these case histories illuminating. They demonstrate the power of the Five Principles, as well as the courage and commitment of those willing to turn their awareness inward to explore, heal, and establish Full Body Presence.

Make a commitment to explore you;
it will transform your life.

Chapter Nine

Guidelines for Living
and Working with Others:
The Gift of Your Presence

If you regularly work with the Five Principles and the Explorations, you will begin to notice a change for the better in yourself — more energy, self-awareness, strength, and more confidence to meet life on your own terms. You have learned that caring for yourself and treating yourself with respect give you more ease and resilience. You don't tire as easily, and you don't fear life's demands. You are able to be present to the demands of others, without feeling overwhelmed or exhausted. You know how to say "no" when appropriate, and you know how to turn inward to nourish yourself and maintain your vitality. And you viscerally understand that you are part of the unconditional sea of energy that surrounds us.

Let us now explore how you can give the gift of your presence to those in your world. Your Full Body Presence matters; the gift of your presence is most potent when you are grounded, connected, and fully present in the face of whatever comes up. Presence allows you to be compassionate without taking on others' pain — maintaining healthy boundaries without losing the energy and the desire to help. Simply put, your energetic presence can have a healing effect on others.

You are learning how to be in touch with and nurture yourself, so that your presence can catalyze and nurture the healing of others. Developing the ability to be a strong therapeutic presence is one of the greatest gifts you can give yourself and those around you, for it connects you more deeply with your world and opens you fully to life. Professional caregivers — such as bodyworkers, counselors, ministers, healthcare practitioners, life coaches, and teachers — are not the only ones who need to nurture themselves and maintain healthy boundaries. All of us are caregivers on some level. We care for our partners, parents, and children, friends, and co-workers, and we volunteer at hospitals, food kitchens, and homeless shelters. So, all of us can benefit from the skills that professional caregivers learn.

I would like to leave you with a set of practical guidelines for serving as a healing presence for others, which have been adapted from guidelines I developed for professional healthcare practitioners. You will see the principles of Full Body Presence woven throughout. Following these precepts will keep you from falling into old patterns and increase the steadiness and strength of your own healing presence. Your confidence in yourself as a healing presence will increase as you practice the skills taught in this book.

Before You Offer Your Healing Presence

Consider the following before you engage with someone in your life who needs your caring presence, whether it's your child or your next-door neighbor or a client.

Take Care of You

Nurture the conviction that you deserve to take care of yourself. This is not only good for those you care for — it is an essential part of your birthright as a human being. "Put your own oxygen mask on first" so that there will be someone to help those in need around you. Changing your attitude to reflect this self-respect can make all the difference in the world.

Check In

Take a reading of where you are on the inside. Scan your body's internal landscape so you'll know if you're energetically full or depleted. If your energy is low, take enough time to ground and fill yourself. This is an excellent thing to do first thing in the morning, so you can plan your day accordingly.

Connect and Fill

Connect to healthy resources; make them habits. Learn what fills and nourishes you so you can engage others with a generous and steady presence. Healthy connection might involve feeling your feet on the ground, the steadiness of the earth, and the nourishing energy it provides. It might mean taking a few slow, nurturing breaths or taking the time to commune with Spirit.

Clearly Set Your Intention

Articulate to yourself what it is you hope to accomplish. For instance, "I want to be present to my son Lenny's fear about football tryouts and to nourish his confidence in whatever ways I can." This does not mean having an agenda for the other person; it does mean respecting boundaries and knowing what you are willing to do.

Affirm Your Current Realities

"I am here today to hold this space for Lenny, to the degree that I can, even though I am tired (or preoccupied, or late for work, or Lenny is being sullen)." Accept the realities of your current circumstances rather than denying them. This enables you to better work with the limitations instead of being tripped up by them.

Remember That You Are Not Alone

Remind yourself that you are not the only resource for those you want to help. Everyone has a variety of friends or counselors and unseen inner and outer support. You are not solely responsible for another person's process. We all live in this sea of energy; trust in it for others as well, even if they cannot feel it right now. Your trust gives you a steadier presence, which can help others remember and connect with their support more easily.

While You Are Offering Your Healing Presence

Consider the following while you are with the person you want to help.

Hold a Space of Compassion and Acceptance

A caring, nonjudgmental attitude that meets others where they are is vital to healing. To do this more easily, bring your Full Body Presence to the situation. Silently repeating a simple prayer, quotation, or poem that inspires your compassion and acceptance is one of many ways you can set your intention and deepen your sense of caring. This Buddhist prayer is one possibility:

> May you be happy.
> May you be peaceful.
> May you be healthy.

One of my other favorites is the "Serenity Prayer" used so widely in twelve-step programs:

God grant me the serenity to accept the things I cannot change,
The courage to change the things I can,
And the wisdom to know the difference.

The paradox of this attitude is that while it may seem on the surface to be one in which nothing gets done, in actuality, when we adopt an attitude of compassion and acceptance, it opens the door to limitless possibilities. The walls of self-judgment come down in the presence of true acceptance and compassion. Self-love can then well up in ways not previously known. And it is in the presence of love that true healing can occur.

Establish Healthy Boundaries

Be a container large enough for the experiences you encounter. Therapeutic presence communicates steadiness and clarity through your body language. This presence says that you welcome and can handle memories, feelings, and experiences that may arise. If you need to say "no" to something, you do. This is what healthy boundaries are about. Until you can say "no," it is difficult to convey a wholehearted "yes" to what is being asked of you.

Establish and maintain clear boundaries. Be present in your own body, and know what your internal landscape feels like. This kind of intimate self-knowledge tells you where your body stops and the other person begins. Learn to clearly differentiate your sensations and emotions from those of the person you are with. Stay within your own body, without energetically leaning into people in order to help; it feels a lot safer and more comfortable for them as well.

Another paradox arises here. Most of us naturally do lean into whomever we are trying to help, but what feels safest to someone in need is a caregiver with Full Body Presence that is wide, diffuse, and not highly focused on them. The steadiness of the caregiver's grounded presence, combined with a wide, noninvasive energy field and nurturing touch are what facilitate healing most effectively. The person in need can then come forward and inform you of what is needed in order to heal. This is a basic CranioSacral principle that applies to life as well.

Be aware when your own emotional issues are being triggered, and know what to do about them. Signs of this might include feeling uncomfortable, needing the person you're with to respond in a certain way (e.g., to be relaxed and comfortable), or needing the person to see you in a certain way (e.g., as the "all-knowing person" who is helping them). All of these signal a hidden agenda on your part. Notice when you are trying to control the outcomes or needing to talk when silence would be golden.

If you discover your own emotional issues coming to the surface in response to the situation you are in, silently recognize them, own them, and, as soon as is appropriate, address them in some way. This might mean using Exploration 3 or working with a therapist or a mentor.

If you are touching the person you are helping, whether casually (a supportive hand on the shoulder or perhaps holding a hand) or therapeutically, listen to what your body, hands, and intuition tell you. As you know by now, our bodies provide us with a magnificent navigational system. As we regain the ability to be more fully in our bodies, we naturally develop our own unique set of receptors that inform us about others' physical, emotional, and spiritual states. Learning to read the signals from this rich navigational system might include listening to your gut feeling about someone, sensing an emotion that is about to bubble up in someone before it is actually expressed, or feeling drawn to an area of the body that you sense is in pain or needs your attention. You can then take action appropriate to your role with this person (a parent might be a comforting presence, whereas a healthcare provider might be taking a therapeutic action).

When Using Touch in a Professional Treatment

When you are using touch in a professional treatment, keep the following guidelines in mind.

Tune In to the Person You Are Touching

Let the body of the person you are with tell you what it needs. You can do this by quietly asking yourself: What is the quality of energy under my hands — does his or her energy meet me and soak up what I have to offer easily, or does it initially push me away? Where is energy flowing or not flowing? Are there other images that come up when I lay my hands on this person's body, such as a fullness, an emptiness, colors, textures, a different resonance? And remember not to censor the incoming information.

Witness without an Agenda

Listen carefully to what is said during the time you are together. Listen quietly; make soft, affirmative sounds to acknowledge that you hear the other person. You might gently paraphrase back what was said to be sure you heard correctly. Simply being witnessed by another human being in this way is deeply healing in and of itself.

Honor Their Process and Pace

Honor the process and pace of the person you're working with — whether you are listening to someone's story about growing up with his mother's mental illness or helping a client deal with the pain of multiple miscarriages. If you're holding a healing space for another's most ingrained and painful internal knot — one they've carried around for years — it may well take more time to fully heal. Deep-seated physical and emotional tensions usually take longer to resolve. It is not your job to judge the unfolding or pace of another's healing, but rather to be present for the healing that can happen in this moment. If you try to push too hard for resolution of an issue with many layers that have built up over years, you will most likely end up feeling exhausted and depleted, and the person you are trying to help will feel pushed or won't be able to fully integrate the work that you have done. Do what you can now, and let the rest go.

Hold a Larger Vision

Maintain a vision of the person you are with as whole and healthy. At times, it may be appropriate to help the person remember how far they have come when they are feeling discouraged. This is as true for a child struggling in school with a learning disability as it is for an adult with chronic pain. It can be challenging to hold a vision of someone as healthy and whole when the problems are severe and multifaceted. But it is essential that you do so. Learning to see that person's full potential and capacity to heal is one of the greatest gifts you can give.

Holding a space for possible healing does not mean having a Pollyanna attitude or giving false hope. It means recognizing that our innate capacity to heal is an unknown. I have seen remarkable healing take place that by all rights should not have been possible. So, I never want to close the door to that possibility in someone's mind. I also recognize that healing to a dying patient may look like that person's coming to terms with his life and dying peacefully — not healing his physical body.

Empower Them

Help the person you are with to get in touch with his or her own capacity for self-healing and empowerment. Your role is to be a compassionate witness, a loving guide. You can create the conditions in which healing may occur, but you are not the healer. The ultimate gift you can give is to help others uncover their own capacity to heal themselves. As they release tension and trauma from their tissues, they will naturally get more in touch with the things that nurture and nourish them in life and will begin to make healthier choices.

After You Have Been Present for Another

After offering someone your healing presence, you can close the session in the following ways.

Recognize Their Changes

When you conclude, ask how the person is feeling on a physical, a mental, and an emotional level. In the process of talking together, you will be teaching them to pay attention to the subtle inner signals they need to discover and discern for themselves. For instance, as a parent, you might ask: "What is your confidence level now about giving that speech?" or, "How are you feeling now about the upcoming basketball game?" As a therapist you might ask: "What can you do differently in your life now, after the work we've just done together?"

As a healthcare practitioner, you might ask: "How is the pain in your hip now, compared to when you came in?" or, "Your headache was a seven when you got here. Where is it now on a scale from one to ten? Has the quality or location of the pain changed?" By asking for specific information, you are helping them notice things they might have discounted before. You are empowering them to listen more effectively to their own internal landscape and bring it into their lives.

Acknowledge Their Commitment

Acknowledge their courage and commitment to heal. This can help them feel less passive and more like proactive partners in their own healing process. This is particularly important when someone is feeling discouraged by setbacks or slow progress.

Guide Them to See the Whole Picture

Help them stay aware of the bigger picture. Note the changes you see in them each time you are together, as compared with their earlier distress. Share any progress you have observed. People need feedback when they are not yet able to sense the shifts you are picking up. Often, when I point out some long-term changes to a client at the end of a session, they are pleasantly surprised, "Oh, yeah, that is true. I just wasn't paying attention to that." As teachers or parents, we are in a perfect position to hold and remind our students or children of the larger screen of their lives and how they are progressing through it.

Help Them Plan Follow-up Care

Make suggestions for supplemental or follow-up work if appropriate — such as using the processes and exercises taught in this book. You might recommend journaling or a dream group. This might include your willingness to get together again or referrals to other practitioners — psychotherapists, acupuncturists, and other healthcare practitioners can be helpful in following through, supporting, or bringing to completion this person's healing process.

Hold an Attitude of Gratitude and Acceptance

Close with an attitude of gratitude and acceptance. This will help you stay in the present moment, rather than being caught up in regrets about things you didn't do or worries about what might happen. Acknowledge what you have done well, note the changes you would make if you see each other again in this context, and then let go of what is beyond your capacity to do at this time.

Remember Full Body Presence

Take care of yourself. Remember to end your time together with you feeling full. This might mean taking a few minutes to breathe deeply and feel the earth supporting and filling you up. It might mean closing with a silent prayer of appreciation for the healing and relaxation that has just transpired. It might also mean eating a snack, taking a short break, a walk, or a relaxing bath. When you take care of you first, you are able to be fully present for others.

Therapeutic Presence in the Emergency Room

I recently heard from a friend, an emergency care physician who attended my Full Body Presence: Grounding and Healthy Boundaries training several years ago: "Suzanne, had an interesting experience with a patient tonight in the ER — call me!"

Naturally, I was intrigued, and minutes later we were talking. He told me that a nineteen-year-old girl had been brought in by her parents, unable to stop belching. It was continual, with only seconds between each burp. It had impaired her speech for days and was getting worse. She was quite upset.

After running all the proper tests to rule out more serious issues, my physician friend sat her down and asked her if she was willing to try something with him. She said she'd try anything, so the doctor took a moment to consciously remember his own grounding and Full Body Presence. Then he proceeded to guide her to breathe through her nose rather than her mouth. Between his calm presence and her breathing, things in her body started to relax within minutes. He then slowly and calmly offered a series of suggestions that led her deeper into her body. Ultimately, he got her awareness down to the ground under her, connecting her to the rich energy field of the earth and its relaxing and energizing qualities (he was using a shortened version of Exploration 2).

Fifteen minutes passed as he held his Full Body Presence — and offered her access to her own. "Suzanne," he told me, "it was startling to see how easily and quickly her whole system relaxed and let go as I talked, right there in the ER!" By the time he was finished, she was smiling. And she was no longer belching. Then he let her know that she could do this for herself anytime she needed it. He referred her to resources that would enable her to replicate what they'd just done, and off she went, healthier and happier.

A calm, strong therapeutic presence is valuable in a variety of situations, even some that we might not ordinarily think of. But here's what's key: It needs to be enough of a habit for you that it's easily accessible, even in the toughest situations. It's the being state that helps any technique work more effectively.

Therapeutic Presence with Special-Needs Children and Their Parents

Kathleen, a pediatric speech pathologist with a successful practice in my area, told me this story:

> One of my most difficult, low-functioning little patients, Gina, was brought in last week having the tantrum of all tantrums. Her mom was agitated and uncomfortable, and her little brother was cranky and irritable as well. I often see this with the families of special-needs children who have loud tantrums as a way of expressing their frustrations. It is part of the child's coping mechanism because of their inability to regulate themselves. The parents and siblings of these children often feel embarrassed and don't know what to do in response to this disruptive behavior.
>
> Because I had just come back from one of your trainings, I decided to try something additional in Gina's session. Once I got Gina on my lap, I used your grounding and filling to create Full Body Presence for myself so I could be a strong, steady presence in the room. First, I felt more relaxed, and then everyone else seemed to feel it as well. The deeper and wider I made my energetic field of presence, the more Gina calmed down. First, she stopped crying. Then she made beautiful eye contact, and we had several moments of meaningful, purposeful interaction, which she had never done before.
>
> Next, her brother, who normally demands his share of the attention when she gets agitated, became uncharacteristically calm and went off in a corner to play quietly with the toy trains. Usually, he

would be dragging every toy across the room, expecting everyone to engage with him. Later in the session, we were actually able to include him in our interactions. It is a huge therapeutic step for a child like Gina to have allowed this.

To top it all off, the mom completely relaxed and was smiling by the time they left. Later, she called to tell me that the three of them had a stress-free afternoon, which is unheard of for them.

The only variable that was different in Gina's session that day was that I added a conscious practice of grounding and filling throughout our therapy hour. I now incorporate my Full Body Presence into every session I do. The parents of my patients have started to tell me that I consistently get a lot more done with their children than any of their other therapists. It is amazing how something as simple as grounding and filling can change the outcome of every session. This practice has made my life and my work more effective and easier all at the same time!

Practicing the principles of therapeutic presence takes patience and ongoing commitment, but it is well worth the effort. It opens up a new model, or paradigm of conscious awareness for helping others. Our lives are richest when we can be present to others in each moment, in a space of caring and compassion that enables us to receive as well as give. As an added bonus, the ability to serve as a presence for someone else's healing brings us into a deeper state of grace and resonance.

Everyone receives from this equation.
In this paradigm, to give is indeed to receive.

Chapter Ten

Healing for Today:
A World at Peace

In this closing chapter, use all the skills you have learned in this book to allow yourself to embody the vision that follows. Set your intention for the future from deep inside the present moment of Full Body Presence. As you do this, you may find that your vision is different from mine. Record your vision. Drink it in. Receive it as fully as possible, and then live in accordance with it. Be an agent for change in the direction of your larger vision. Each of us has specific gifts, which are meant to be shared. Find yours and share. Then walk in your world with heartful courage, strength, and tenderness. And enjoy!

Read the following aloud if possible:

Imagine a world where you get up in the morning with energy to meet your day after a good night's rest.

Imagine you begin the day by checking in to make sure your energy reservoir is as full as it can be.

Imagine your curiosity leading your day, so that your options stay
open to whatever resources are available.
Imagine your heart having as much of a voice as your linear thought
processes.
Imagine how it would be to feel steady and sure of yourself as you
make decisions throughout your day.

Imagine being comfortable with *all* of yourself — feeling at home in
your body and your world.
Imagine clarity of mind-body-spirit that guides your direction in the
world — choosing from possibilities that not only feed you but
also that are good for the rest of your world.
Imagine greeting the unfamiliar by being curious, awake, interested
— but not fearful.
Imagine following your curiosity and creating in your world using
your natural gifts.

If you are not feeling well, imagine having the presence to check in
with yourself and be a detective in your system so that you can
get the best care possible.
Imagine knowing the questions to ask and getting the care you need.
Imagine taking the time to heal fully.

Imagine an ability to be friends with time — to slow down and enjoy
your day, to rest and rejuvenate, *and* to effortlessly speed up and
go for the goal when that is needed.
Imagine, as you meet the day, that you respond from inside your system. Your deeper creativity is acted upon.
Imagine you operate from a deep sense of love rather than a fear of
change or others who are different from you.

Imagine being able to feel the tenderness in your heart and not being
afraid of it.
Imagine feeling strong enough to feel what is in your heart and ex-
press it.

Imagine allowing your world to touch you deeply, drinking in the
beauty that is around you — being able to soak up the love that
is in your environment, rather than letting it pass by.

Imagine trusting your body and treating it like a valued friend and ally.
Imagine listening to, responding to, and following through with its
care and healing.
Imagine allowing yourself to slow down and rest when you need it.
Imagine taking the time to enjoy your world — to celebrate and play.

Imagine feeling the strength and power of your lower body and
being comfortable with it — in fact, imagine deeply enjoying it.
Imagine having the wisdom to walk in your world with both your
power and your tenderness.
Imagine being able to sense what kind of movement would be most
healing and energizing.
Imagine feeling inspired to move in that way, rather than having to
force yourself to exercise.
Imagine having your sexuality be a healthy, integrated part of you.
Imagine feeling comfortable with your sensuality — giving nurtur-
ing touch in your life and happily receiving it.
Imagine a world where healing bodywork is readily available.

Imagine feeling deeply connected — a part of your environment.
Imagine valuing the natural world like a trusted family member.
Imagine a world where all decisions take the young, the old, and
those without a voice into account; where even the smallest of
things are considered; where resources other than money and
size are the important deciding factors in any given moment.

Imagine a world where you are trusted and trustworthy.
Imagine a world that operates on trustworthiness — where it is held
in high esteem; where you learn to trust yourself and know how
to trust others; and where you know from your inner gut feeling
when something is really off or absolutely right on.

Imagine a world where, from a young age, you are helped to find your natural gifts and talents.

Imagine a world where you are then encouraged to explore and develop those gifts and talents as you grow.

Imagine a world where people become parents when they are ready, have the skills, and are supported in raising their children by their communities.

Imagine a world where people have access to the resources that nourish them — where they remember to slow down and take more time off periodically to feed their spirit, to *sense into* what is best for their higher good.

Imagine a world where people have the freedom and resources to join with others who are of like spirit and mind, to reconnect and rejuvenate at that level.

Imagine a world where people honor spiritual differences and learn from them.

Imagine a world where excellent health care is available when you need it, where open communication with your own body is reflected in the larger system, and where your healthcare providers include your inner wisdom in their plan for your care.

Imagine a world where international relations are built on the deeper understanding that we are all connected and that to survive and thrive, we must respond to each other knowing that what truly helps one must help the other as well.

Imagine a world where we also have this understanding about our environment — where we treasure it, treat it with care and respect.

Imagine a world where our food, air, earth, and water resources are pure, where they support healthy bodies and minds.

Imagine a world where our media systems — television, movies, the Internet — educate us about what is healthy and help us to listen inside, where we are encouraged to find our own unique gifts and style.

Imagine a world where the government is truly looking out for each person's well-being, the well-being of the environment, and the education and happiness of the people as a whole — where special interests are balanced and weighed against the good of the whole.

Imagine a system where your voice is heard and your vote matters.

Imagine the joy of living in Full Body Presence.

*Now that you have imagined all of this,
go out and live it. And enjoy!*

Acknowledgments

It has taken a village to write this book. I am an oral tradition person, and making the shift from speaking to writing has been a huge task for me. In doing this, an entire village of friends, colleagues, family, students, and teachers have helped me bring this book forward. It has been a project that has spanned a decade and taken many forms along the way. I want to remember and honor everyone who has contributed in large and small ways along the path, so here goes.

My first thanks must go to Kari Uman for helping me write my initial version of the Five Principles and Peggy Linden for helping me write my first study guide — both invaluable beginning steps. Then there were a series of excellent writers who midwifed my writing process at different points along the way — thank you to Kim Falone, Kay Schaefer, Jodi Carlson, Carol Goldsmith, Lulu Torbet, Maureen O'Neill, Laura Davis, and my final book-birthing writer, Ja-lene Clark. And thanks to my original illustrator, Kay Hansen, and my designer and illustrator for this book, David Andor. Right behind these are my instructors and presenters, many of whom donated hours to days poring over the materials to help me clarify and organize. So, a *huge* thanks goes out to Joanna Haymore, Kathy Burns, Angela Stevens, Lori Chinitz, Amelia Mitchell, Cari Rowan, Gene Miller, Dale Kressley,

Richard Griffin, Sandy Brown, Deb Schneider-Murphy, and Tamara Blossic.

The rest of the village — some who donated a lot of time brainstorming or editing my writing at key points in this process — get my next wave of gratitude. A huge thank-you goes to the loving efforts of my women's group (you know who you are), Jane Luce, Karen Hale, Kay Shubert, Karen Copeland, John Hoernemann, Chris Slate, Susie Steiner, Tim Hutton, Maryalice Fischer, Cheri Bailey, Connie Wells, Christi Fath, Diana Walker, Julie Johns, Deb Wahl, Laura Mitchell, Cosper Scafidi, Carol Duffner, and Donna Setzer.

I am sure there are others I am forgetting. It has been a decade of asking for and receiving help from my entire village. Thank you all from the bottom of my heart.

I could not have completed this book without my dedicated Healing from the Core office team's efforts to keep it all running across the last decade: Lynn (and Tim) Foley, Jan Yates, B. J. Frame, Robin Heimburg, Cynthia Schell, Deb Krahling, Monique Roberts, Carol Molesky, and Elizabeth Charles. Some of you actually had a desk in the office and others supported me from behind the scenes; nonetheless you all were wonderful — thanks!

Then the next great wave of gratitude goes out to all the students and clients whose experiences have enriched my life and this book. Your stories have taught me valuable lessons that were passed forward here.

And, finally, the biggest wave of gratitude goes to my family members who have supported and encouraged me throughout this entire process — my husband, Carlos; my daughter, Alieza; my son, Aren; my mother, Mary Jane; and my sister, Debbie. Your patience and love (and shoulder massages) have been invaluable resources for me. You keep me going. I love you all.

Appendix

Transcriptions of Audio Explorations

Introduction

The following audio program accompanies the book *Full Body Presence: Learning to Listen to Your Body's Wisdom* by Suzanne Scurlock-Durana. In this program, Suzanne presents three Explorations — the directions for how to use them optimally are in the book.

* *As a reminder, do not listen to any of these Explorations while driving a car or operating other heavy machinery, as these Explorations lead listeners into a deep state of relaxation and may cause drowsiness.*

To download the free audio tracks for this book or order a CD for a small fee plus shipping, visit

www.healingfromthecore.com,
click on the Full Body Presence Download link,
and enter the password *presence*

or write to us at

Healing from the Core
P.O. Box 2534
Reston, VA 20195-2534

TRANSCRIPT OF EXPLORATION 1
Opening Awareness:
Where Am I in This Moment?

Welcome to Exploration 1, Opening Awareness — "Where Am I in *This* Moment?"

My name is Suzanne Scurlock-Durana, and I'll be your guide throughout this series.

Begin by settling in, gliding into neutral, releasing your expectations, agendas, and judgments. Allow yourself to naturally, effortlessly respond to the following suggestions and questions, knowing that the ideal response is whatever spontaneously shows up in your body and your conscious awareness as we go. The nature of your experience will naturally change and deepen as this process unfolds and with repeated practice.

Choose a comfortable seat with good back support and let your feet rest easily and fully on the floor. Take a moment now to get comfortable and then we'll begin.

[Pause]

As you close your eyes or partially close your eyes, turning your attention inward, gather your awareness, your openness to discovery, and let it travel in with your breath, following your inhalation down into your lungs . . . settling your conscious awareness inside your body — and letting the external world fall away. . . .

Let's begin by taking a baseline reading, an overall look, inwardly scanning your entire body from head to toe, being curious about anything that pops into your awareness, noting areas that feel at ease, comfortable — in other words, where you feel more connection. You may notice sensations of warmth or coolness, a sense of fullness or spaciousness; allow yourself to take in these sensations, no matter how subtle. Take a few moments now to notice any area or areas where you feel more connection.

[Pause for fifteen seconds.]

Then notice the internal areas that feel less present, where there is less sensation, or perhaps pain, or numbness. Just notice without judgment. You may notice discomfort or a lack of feeling. Certain areas just may simply feel more distant. Notice anywhere that you feel less connected right now. Internally scanning, relaxed.

[Pause for fifteen seconds.]

You are taking a baseline sensory snapshot of how you feel overall as you begin.

[Pause for fifteen seconds.]

Now bring your attention back to your breath and allow yourself to be curious about the subtle sensations of breathing. Notice the temperature of the air as it enters your nose and throat, traveling down into your lungs. Is it cool or warm? Feel the rise and fall of your ribs. Is there anywhere that your breathing feels restricted, or is it easy and full?

As you inhale and exhale, do you notice your chest rising and falling, or are you more aware of your back resting against the chair? In other words, is more of you present right now in the front of you or in the back? Or do you feel them both equally?

Allow your attention to move up into your neck and head. What do they feel like?

What do your eyes feel like? Is there any sense of strain or are they relaxed? How does the air around you feel on your cheeks?

What does your mouth feel like? Is your jaw tight or relaxed? How do your teeth and gums and tongue feel? Hmmm.

How does your neck feel right now? Does one side feel more relaxed than the other? How does your throat feel?

Returning to your chest, notice your breathing again for a moment. With your deepening awareness, do you notice any changes? How does the rise and fall of your ribs feel now? Hmmm.

How does your heart feel? Allow yourself to feel the sensations in your heart area with as little interpretation as possible. Can you feel it beating? Be aware of all the different ways you receive sensation. Does your heart feel like a particular color?

And letting your attention spread out from the heart area, allow yourself to notice the sensations in the rest of your chest . . . and on out to your shoulders . . . your upper back . . . down your arms into your hands and fingers. How do your arms and hands feel? Heavy or light? Distant or connected to your chest and heart? Pulsating or vibrating? How do your arms and hands feel right now?

When you are ready, allow your attention to return to your breath, letting your awareness drop down as you exhale, settling into your torso, deeper and wider with each exhale . . . noticing. Does one side of your torso feel denser or lighter than the other? Bigger or smaller? Or are things balanced equally? Is there a particular texture or color or pulsation that you sense anywhere in your torso? Hmmm.

Do you have a sense of your backbone leaning against the chair? Do you feel more up in your neck area or lower down in your sacrum? Or does your energy feel the same throughout? Allow yourself to move gently, if you wish, in order to feel more in your spine. Does your spine feel solid and steady, or is there less sensation here? Notice how connected you feel to the bones of your spine right now. No judgment. Simply noticing . . . good.

Now allow your attention to drop down to your pelvis, to your connection to the chair you're sitting on. What is the sensation of your sitting bones contacting the chair? Is one side resting more fully than the other, or are they balanced equally?

Notice the sensation in your upper legs, of your thighs resting on the chair. Do they feel connected to your body? Can you sense the bones of your thighs?

And your knees? Do they feel different from each other or the same? Stiff or flexible? Do you sense any particular colors or textures?

How about your calves? What do they feel like? Do you have a sense of them being a long way from your head and torso, or do they feel connected and strong? Do they feel alike, or is one more relaxed than the other? Or denser than the other?

How do your feet feel? Notice if the sensations are different or the same for both feet. What do your toes feel like? Do you feel your heels as keenly as you feel the arches and balls of your feet? Are both feet resting easily and fully on the floor, or does one feel more connected than the other? Simply noticing . . . good.

Now take a moment to scan through your entire system again, taking another overall broadbrush look at your internal landscape, as you did when you began. As your awareness deepens, what are you noticing? Are there any changes since you first scanned your body? Take note of any sensory information: colors, textures, areas of dark or lightness, symmetries or asymmetries. Being curious and simply noticing . . .

When you are done, let your awareness return to the outer world. Gently open your eyes and notice how the world around you feels now, compared to when you began. And thank yourself for taking this time to deepen your internal awareness.

To download the free audio tracks for this book or order a CD
for a small fee plus shipping, visit

www.healingfromthecore.com,
click on the Full Body Presence Download link,
and enter the password *presence*

or write to us at

Healing from the Core
P.O. Box 2534
Reston, VA 20195-2534

TRANSCRIPT OF EXPLORATION 2

Grounding and Filling: Nourishing and Replenishing the Container of Your Being

Let yourself begin by settling in. And as this process unfolds, allow yourself to naturally, effortlessly respond to the following suggestions and questions, knowing that the ideal response is whatever spontaneously shows up in your body and in your conscious awareness as we go. Exploration 2 is the core practice of the embodiment process. The nature of your experience will naturally change and deepen with repeated practice.

Again, make yourself comfortable, with your eyes closed or partially closed and your feet resting easily and fully on the floor. And again, invite your curiosity, your openness to discovery, to lead your conscious awareness in this Exploration, so you can release any expectations or judgments as you go.

Following your breath, allow your awareness to drop into your internal landscape, feeling the rise and fall of your rib cage with each inhale . . . and exhale . . . breathing normally and noticing the sensations . . . the temperature of the air in your nostrils, the feel of the air traveling down into your lungs, your chest rising and falling, the feeling of your backbone on the chair. Simply noticing . . . being curious.

Where are you more present in your body in this moment and where are you not — where there is ease and comfort or . . . numbness or pain? Take a sensory snapshot that gives you a beginning reference point.

Breathing comfortably, allow your awareness to drop on down through your torso. Are your sitting bones resting equally on the chair?

How do your knees feel today? Hmmm.

How do your feet feel resting on the floor? Simply notice; no judgment.

[Pause]

Now we are going to make contact with the earth, right down through the floor and into the ground, connecting with its rich and abundant energy. Allow your awareness to drop down beneath your feet, into the earth's field as though you were putting down roots of awareness, or perhaps light beams of awareness, or maybe riding a river of awareness — use whichever imagery works for you. What does the earth feel like under you? Let sensations come without judgment. Is it cool or warm? Is it hard-packed and rocky? Or are you moving through sand or loose soil? Give yourself permission to take in these sensations, even if you don't know exactly where they're coming from.

Now allow your awareness to go deeper into the earth, as though there is no resistance. Traveling down your roots or light beams or flowing on your river of awareness — going as deeply as it feels comfortable for you right now. [Pause] Perhaps your roots are on their way to the core of the earth, or you may be spreading a carpet of tiny roots right on the earth's surface. Or in this moment you may just be able to feel the earth touching your feet, but may not yet be comfortable extending your awareness down into it. Wherever you are is fine. Simply notice what sensations show up when you get curious as to what the earth feels like under you. [Pause] Allow yourself to notice that you can feel this connection outside of yourself that's safe, unconditional, and supportive.

And, if you are feeling any excess tension, give yourself permission to simply let it go. You can take a deep breath and exhale the tension [inhale and exhale deeply]. Or you can allow it to flow like water, down and out into the earth. Or you can release it through the pores of your skin, like moisture evaporating on a cool breeze. Simply allowing yourself to let go of whatever excess tension you may have, whatever you no longer need.

Hmmm. And now, setting the intention to receive only what is most nurturing and nourishing, starting at your feet, invite the earth's energy field to begin to fill your body — your container — by asking yourself, "What would feel most nurturing and nourishing in my feet right now?"

Warmth or coolness? Do you feel a deep pulsation or maybe a high-pitched humming? Be alert to all sensory cues. Hmmm.

Does it feel like a particular color? Perhaps a cool blue-green or a warm red-orange or some other color?

Allow your feet to gently fill, letting nurturing sensation come up through the earth and in through your skin, soaking into all your muscles, ligaments, and tendons, letting every cell fill, all the way into the very core of your bone marrow and all the way out to your skin. Bones are like sturdy sponges, filled with many tiny air spaces. So allow your bones to soak up this nurturing, nourishing energy as though they were sponges soaking up clean, clear water.

Your feet may feel like they are becoming longer and wider as they fill. You may notice that one foot fills more fully or a little more quickly than the other. Or you may simply experience an increased awareness — as you intend to let your feet receive nurturing sensation, they may simply feel different. Do your best not to judge how much or how little you may be feeling.

Let your curiosity come forward and then notice what sensations show up.

Moving at a pace that works for you, invite that nourishing feeling up into your ankles. Again, allow the sensation to soak all the way into your bones and all the way out to your skin. Hmmm.

How about your shins and calves? What would feel most nurturing there? Coolness or warmth, pulsating or humming? Perhaps the sensation — the feeling — of a long, slow stretch? Allow yourself to receive whatever sensation would nourish your calves and shins right now . . . letting all your cells fill up and plump out — feeling juicy.

What would feel most healing and energizing in your knees? Let that sensation permeate all the nooks and crannies of your knees, soaking up this replenishing energy.

And, as we go along, if there is an area that has a harder time receiving nurturing sensation, simply notice it, allow that place to receive what it can, and cradle it gently with your awareness. Then move on, always going at your own pace.

How about your thighs? Allow this nourishing sensation to soak from the bone marrow of your thighs all the way out to your skin ... letting it flow from the earth up through your feet and calves and knees right into your thighs. Good.

Allow a sense of safe, nurturing sensation to begin to fill your pelvis. What would feel most nourishing and healing to your sitting bones, your hip bones, your sacrum — that V-shaped bone at the base of your spine, the entire pelvic bowl ... soaking up this nourishment like a sponge in a clear pool of water. [Sound of soaking up]

And what would feel most nurturing and energizing in your belly? Take a nice deep breath, cradle this area with your awareness, and let it fill and relax. Allow yourself to experience this area, because there's plenty of wonderful energy to be awakened here.

Yes, you may feel the area around and under your navel, gently opening, filling up from your legs, into your belly, and then moving all the way back to your spine, and all the way out to your sides. Letting all your reproductive organs and the other organs of your belly and midsection soak up what they need to feel energized and relaxed and full of life. Hmmm.

And if you notice your mind wandering for a moment, simply bring your attention back — *Oh, yes, I was nurturing my belly* — *taking the time to slow down and nurture myself.*

Let this flow of nourishing energy permeate your spine. . . . Is it warm or cool? Does it feel like a particular color? Notice as each vertebra, all the way up, and the spinal cord inside the vertebral canal, soak up whatever would feel most healing and relaxing right now. Hmmm.

It's helpful to breathe easily and as deeply as you can during this phase, because the breath moves the spine from the inside out and gives you more sensory awareness of it. [Inhale and exhale.] Also, feeling your spine against the chair or whatever is supporting you gives you even more sensory information about your backbone.

If you find any area where there is pain, you may notice that for a moment or two the pain intensifies. If so, just simply allow yourself to be with it as best you can. You're not trying to change or force the pain out; you're just gently sitting with it and allowing it to receive whatever nurturing and nourishing energy it can in this moment. And you may find that where the rest of your body wants a rosy red color, an area that's in pain may seem to want some other color, perhaps a nice cool blue, green, or a clear silver color. Allow it to soak up whatever nurturing it can.

Now, what would feel most nurturing in your chest, your lungs, and your heart? Perhaps the sense of an easy full breath [inhale and exhale], bringing fresh oxygen to your lungs and then your heart and on out to all your cells as you inhale and exhale. [Inhale and exhale audibly.] Hmmm. Nice.

And what would feel most relaxing and energizing to your shoulders . . . your upper chest and back? I often summon the feeling of snuggling in a soft blanket. What would feel most nourishing to you right here in your shoulders right now?

[Pause]

Continue to relax and receive the sensations of nourishing yourself, taking in only what is most nurturing to you right now. Often your mind doesn't know the answer when you ask internally — and yet a sensation shows up that feels relaxing or energizing or nurturing. Simply open and receive it as best you can. Hmmm.

And what would feel most relaxing and energizing in your arms, your upper arms, your elbows, your forearms, down into your hands? You can gently let your fingers stretch out to draw the nurturing flow down your arms into your hands and fingers. Hmmm.

And what would feel most nourishing to your neck and throat?

Coolness or warmth? Perhaps a sensation of spaciousness or movement? What would feel most healing and energizing here? Allow yourself to receive it as fully as you can right now. Hmmm.

What about your face, your jaw, your eyes? What sensation would feel most relaxing and nurturing here? Hmmm.

Allow that nurturing sensation to filter all the way through to the back of your head, filling and relaxing your entire brain, all the membranes and surrounding structures and bones, filling and being energized.

Tune in to this flow of nurturing energy filling you . . . filling all of you . . . coming in from the earth under you, through your feet and legs, through your torso and neck, arms and hands, all the way up into your head, filling and nurturing you all the way up to the crown of your head . . . until it begins to move out the crown, showering down around you like a gentle fountain, bathing your skin and the energy field that runs through it and around it.

If your head feels a little closed at the top, like a slight sensation of pressure, gently and slowly pull up on your hair right there at the crown, or rub your head until you feel it open, allowing that river of energy to flow out, showering down around you.

So we're nearing the end of this Exploration.

[Pause]

When you're ready, gently notice how you feel now compared to when you began. Simply notice.

You've just connected, grounding into the earth, receiving its nourishment and support. You have created a fuller, stronger energy field within yourself, and bathed in it for quite a while. You have strengthened your personal boundaries, the membrane between you and the world. This allows you to connect more deeply when you choose to and to feel strong enough to say "no" when you need to. It gives you clarity to see yourself and the world around you and the energy to cope with whatever arises. Notice how you feel now compared to when you began. This nourishing energy is always available to you through this process and is your core access to building a strong, nurturing container for your own life's energy and pleasure.

And when you're ready, bring your awareness back from the internal to the external. Feel your feet on the floor as you open your eyes. Allow yourself to drink in your surroundings, being informed and nurtured by all you see.

Yes, good, enjoy!

To download the free audio tracks for this book or order a CD
for a small fee plus shipping, visit

www.healingfromthecore.com,
click on the Full Body Presence Download link,
and enter the password *presence*

or write to us at

Healing from the Core
P.O. Box 2534
Reston, VA 20195-2534

TRANSCRIPT OF EXPLORATION 3
Healing the Internal Resistance to Life

Welcome to Exploration 3. This Exploration is done in three segments. You may stop after any of the three segments or go all the way through. The first segment explores a physical place of resistance, the second segment addresses limiting beliefs and painful recurring thoughts, and the third segment is on healing relationships. They are in this order because they build on each other. You will be given the option to stop the session at the end of each segment (signaled by a ten-second silence), or you can cruise on through the entire Exploration.

So make yourself comfortable, with good back support and your feet planted easily and fully on the floor, readjusting your position as needed during the process, eyes closed or slightly open. Allow your mind to glide into neutral, releasing any expectations, agendas, or judgments you may be aware of right now. As best you can, let yourself simply experience this process.

Take a couple of easy breaths, settling back into your body. Scan through your whole internal landscape, noticing all the sensations and textures, easily filling and energizing, connecting to the earth or whatever unconditional resource works best for you at this time, so that you are beginning this Exploration full and energized.

[Pause]

[Slowly] Now, bring to your awareness the area of your body where you feel most at home, where you feel a strong sense of connection. It might be your heart or your belly. It might be your feet, or your pelvis, or your hands. It could be your backbone. Wherever you feel the strongest sense of presence, let your awareness go and rest in that place right now and feel the fullness, the strength of that place. It will probably feel very comfortable to be there. It is easy to rest into this place.

Take a moment now to soak up a little more from the earth's field of energy, allowing nourishing sensation into this area, so that it begins to expand and spread out.

And in this place of strength and presence, let yourself feel or see or sense a ball of healing presence or energetic healing hands, emitting energy that is loving, patient, nurturing, strong, yet soft. This place contains unconditional love for you, which you may feel as comfort or support in some way. So, if energy hands feel right for you, use that. If a ball of healing presence works best for you, work with that image.

Sense or feel or see this healing energy in whatever way you can. Sometimes you just know that it's there. Even if you don't know how you know, that's fine. Some of you will be able to vividly see this healing presence or your energy hands; you'll have a color, a pulsation, a texture. Some of you will clearly feel this healing presence. You'll feel the warmth and strength. Simply allow yourself to have an awareness of this energy presence, in whatever way you can. Yes . . . good.

Next, ask to be shown what block or place of resistance in your body would be best for you to work with today. Notice what pops into your conscious awareness after you've asked. It may be a surprise to you, or it may be a familiar place, a place where you've often felt resistance or pain. You may feel a restricted sensation in this place or a sense of disconnection from the energy flow in the surrounding areas. You may know exactly where this is, or you may need to look around a little, asking your body to show you more clearly. Sometimes there will be pain or numbness there, or maybe it's a place that resonates with a limiting or painful phrase you often hear in your head. Perhaps you experience it as a place of trapped emotion such as grief or rage, sadness or shame. If you discover more than one troubled area, ask to be shown which one would be best for you to work with today. Trust what your body shows you.

Feel the edges of this place. Does it have a color? Does it have a shape? Notice . . . notice . . . What size is it? If it begins to feel overwhelming, let it rest back in your consciousness for a moment, and take your awareness back to your place of greatest strength and comfort, and then down to your feet, tuning up your connection to the unconditional rich energy field of the earth. Good.

When you are ready, allow your awareness to return to that part of you where you feel most at home — and to the ball of healing presence or the energy hands that live in that area of your body where you feel most connected. Allow this healing presence, your energy hands, to expand from your place of strength and to gently cradle the place that feels painful or disconnected or resistant — gently, with no expectations. If your actual physical hands can hold this place easily and without straining, allow them to join your energy hands or presence in cradling this spot.

These hands are not here to change this resistant part of you — your healing presence has no agenda. It is simply loving, caring, and strong — unconditionally holding and loving the part of you that feels disconnected (perhaps feeling hurt, ashamed, or unworthy in some way).

If you are holding a physical sensation of pain, like a lump of grief in your throat, or an area of pain in your heart, or a clutch of fear in your gut, just gently cradle that place and let the pain or the grief or the fear or the shame emerge at its own pace to connect with the healing energy hands or presence. There is no goal to change anything. Your pain and resistance is there for some reason. And perhaps that reason is outdated. There was a valid reason when it began, and it may now be a defense you no longer need. It's not important to understand it now. Simply hold it and love it. Loving in the agape definition of love — all encompassing, unconditional love for yourself, as though you were cradling a sleeping kitten or puppy.

Just gently hold it. You are simply there to be with that aspect of yourself. You are not doing anything to it. You're not going to throw it away. You're not going to try to make it disappear. You are simply there with it.

This can be challenging, particularly if you are holding a place of chronic pain. You may already feel more aware and connected to that painful place than you want to be, habitually feeling the edges of it and managing your day around it. But if you can allow yourself to go deeper today, you'll find that you are not truly connected with this place. You have been holding it at bay, controlling it — in order to be able to tolerate it. So let the edges of the pain just gently be with those energy hands or that healing presence. Simply be present, connecting with the pain, with the grief, with the sadness, whatever it is.

And if you start to feel overwhelmed by the emotion or the pain, let it take a backseat for a moment and return to feeling your feet on the ground, feeling the energy flowing up through your body, backing up the support of your healing energy hands or presence, restoring the strong, safe container around the process, around this issue that's going on. And when you're ready, return to gently cradling it, noticing what happens. Noticing what happens as you hold it. No expectations. Often, this is the hardest part. Your mind may have a different agenda that sounds like this:

"Oh, but I want to get rid of it."

"Oh, but I'm so tired of this pain."

"Oh, I hate this feeling."

Whatever the words are, let them go on by. Let the judgment go and allow yourself to simply be there, connecting more and more with that part as best you can in this moment.

Accepting what is without letting it drive your bus or take over your existence. Reminding yourself that this place of pain or grief is not all of you; it is only a part of you. You also have your feet under you; you have your energy flowing and surrounding this area; you have this strong energy presence holding and loving this part of you as best you can at this point. As best you can. Hmmm.

And as things begin to soften and change, remind yourself to simply be with this place — don't slip into doing something with it.

Remember the unconditional love that you're offering this part of you. Consciously we do not want this pain or emotion, but these are deep, long-held patterns that require our patience and compassion to transform.

In my experience, one of the most effective ways to have pain change in a permanent way is to learn how to find a way to release it from its tightened-down state, unlocking it from its prison. To do this you need to become one with it, to connect with it deeply, so that it can be free to heal.

So check in again.

How is it feeling now?

What's happening?

Hmmm...yes...yes...Notice as things change, as they evolve, honoring your own pace, holding that place in your awareness, cradling and loving it unconditionally, allowing whatever arises to unfold. Don't stand in the way. If you notice the edges of your painful place starting to spread out and disperse, let it happen — widen your cradling presence, creating a larger space for it, so that it can evolve and transform when it is ready. Staying connected to it, but allowing it to heal and change at its own pace, so integration is more complete when it finally occurs. Hmmm...yeah.

And notice how this place feels now compared to when you began this process. Allow yourself to notice the small subtle changes as well as the big ones. Just simply being with this place with gratitude for all the healing, large and small, that may have occurred here today.

And, gently let this place know that you will continue to hold it with loving presence, even though your conscious awareness may be elsewhere. And let this part of you know that you have made a commitment to reconnect with it and that your internal healing presence, your energy hands, will stay with this place as long as is required to heal and transform and reconnect with the rest of you...until it is completely integrated, whether that process takes a few minutes or a few months or a few years. You are now committed to healing and integrating this part of you back into the whole.

Segment 2:
Working with Limiting Beliefs

Now let's work with the way in which your mind and, specifically, your limiting beliefs and painful thoughts come into this process. Most of us are aware of the inner critical voice that can plague us with doubting, shaming, chiding, even insulting thoughts, often denigrating our self-worth or questioning our right to exist.

To begin, bring to mind one of your painful thoughts or limiting beliefs — perhaps the one associated with the physical place of resistance that you just held and loved, or notice any limiting or painful thought that is bothering you right now.

Notice where you feel that thought reverberating in your body. Where does it anchor in your system? Oftentimes a very painful thought will reverberate or be anchored in a pretty specific area like your heart, or in a part of your body where you may have chronic pain, or a place that was traumatized at some point in the past, like your throat or belly, or anywhere actually. Simply notice where the connection is between the painful or limiting thought and your body. If it seems to connect to everywhere, notice where the connection seems the strongest or densest. It may be a familiar place.

Wherever the anchor of your pain or discomfort is, allow your internal healing presence, your energy hands, to come and cradle that place as we proceed, loving it as unconditionally as you can in this moment. No agenda. Simply being present with it, holding it gently and witnessing it in the kind, unconditional way you just finished practicing.

Now, silently repeating your limiting belief or painful thought, ask yourself . . .

"Am I sure that this limiting belief is true?"

Can you open to the possibility that this thought is not true at some level?

Really you don't know whether it's true or not; even though you may have a lot of data from past history to back up the fact that it might have been true at some point, you really don't know whether it is still true.

So now ask yourself,

"What would it feel like if I were open to the possibility that this painful thought or limiting belief is not true? What would it feel like?"

And make this question very specific to whatever your painful thought is. For example, if the thought is "I am not good enough," you might say instead,

"I'm open to the possibility that this thought of not being good enough is just not true. I'm open to the possibility that I am good enough."

When you are ready, you can go a step farther and say,

"I'm open to the possibility that not only am I good enough, but that who I am is a pleasure . . . is a pleasure."

Notice how that feels inside when you can say that to yourself and sit with it, believing it, if only for a moment.

Letting all internal judgments go silent.

What does it feel like in your body?

What's the sensation in the area now being cradled by those wonderful energy hands? Notice. Notice.

What would it feel like in your body if you could suspend that limiting belief and feel the ways in which you are a pleasure?

Allow that area to fully receive that possibility, even if it is only for a short while right now. Allow yourself to open even more to that possibility.

[Pause]

What does that feel like? Feeling that you truly are a pleasure.

[Pause]

Can you feel any of the tightness dissipating?

[Pause]

Can you feel more ease in this place?

[Pause]

Can you feel any expansion inside as your perceptual lens expands?

[Pause]

Allow the healing process to unfold. Good.

[Pause]

This process takes positive affirmations all the way to the core of your being, because you are actually feeling in your body — physically sensing — what it is like to open to new possibilities. This allows you to heal not just mentally, but emotionally and physically and, thus, spiritually as well. Good.

And notice how this place feels now compared to when you began this process. Allow yourself to notice the small subtle changes as well as the big ones. Just simply being with this place with gratitude for all the healing, large and small, that may have occurred here today.

And let this place you've been holding and loving — and dialoguing with — gently know that you will continue to hold it with loving presence, even though you may not have it in your conscious awareness as you go on back out into your life.

And, you may want to commit to returning to this Exploration tomorrow and perhaps the next day if something still remains that needs your conscious attention to bring it to completion. So, take a moment and see what commitment, no matter how small, you want to make to yourself in terms of this healing process, and then commit to it for as long as it takes.

Segment 3:

Working with Interpersonal Issues — Relationships

This process also works with issues that are on an interpersonal level. Not surprisingly, stresses and problems in relationships are often the source of great internal pain and discomfort. Right now, you might be carrying around a ball of fear or anger or shame or grief from a fight with your spouse or your teenager, with a work colleague or your best friend. When this occurs, you know that in this relationship something is just not working. The energy is not flowing between you; the connection is not there the way you want it to be.

The following segment will help you shift how you relate to this situation or relationship pattern, starting with your own reactions and moving on to finding new healing possibilities for yourself and perhaps for the other people involved.

Take a moment now to tune up your connection to the earth and make sure you are feeling full and energized.

Next, bring to mind the person, situation or relationship pattern that feels painful or uncomfortable to you right now. As that sinks in, allow yourself to notice the underlying painful thought, the limiting phrase, the internal words that go along with this person or situation. It might be similar to the limiting belief you just worked with or it could be something like,

"I'm just unlovable."

Or "I am not safe."

Or "I feel overwhelmed."

Or "I'm being abandoned."

When a belief like this dominates your thinking, it narrows your perceptual lens, keeping you from feeling the good connections you want to have with this person. Take a moment now and look for the words that reverberate through you to that ball of painful emotion in your body somewhere.

[Pause]

And once again, bring your internal nurturing hands or healing energy presence to that tight place in your body where your limiting belief is anchored and hold it unconditionally and lovingly as you've done in the previous Explorations. Good.

Then begin to expand your perceptual lens on this issue by saying something like,

"I'm open to the possibility that this relationship could be different, that this relationship could heal — could have pleasure in it again. I'm open to the possibility that I could be connected in a healthy way with my husband/teenager/friend/colleague."

Now, the tricky part of this is to hold that possibility, and expand your perceptual lens without letting your left brain jump in immediately trying to problem-solve and figure it all out. Your challenge is to stay in an open feeling state, keeping your expansion and awareness in the realm of possibility, keeping it in the soft, diffuse place where the creativity to resolve the problem will begin to stir and show you the next step in a healing direction, or perhaps even the whole picture.

So you just hold the thought, "I'm open to the possibility. I have no idea what it would look like. Even if in my conscious mind, I cannot imagine how this could be true, I'm open to the possibility that this relationship could heal and be a pleasure again, that it could work, that we could have a connection again around this issue or in this particular area. I don't know how, but I'm open to that possibility."

And then pay attention to what happens in your body. Feel your feet. Feel your torso. Feel your shoulders. Feel the place being cradled by your loving, powerful energy hands. Allow it to shift and change as you feel into this new possibility. Simply cradling it, loving it, and letting go of judgments as they show up.

When you are able to open your perceptual field and you are willing, really willing, to be open to new possibilities, things are bound to unfold in some very interesting ways in your being.

From my own experience, both personally and as a teacher, many long-standing or complex issues, between couples especially, are not so quickly and easily resolved. Sometimes I will need to hold the possibility for healing and reconnection for weeks or months, through many repetitions of this Exploration, before I can really begin to feel in a clear, solid way the direction that I need to go to create that healing, because my resistance and my ego are so strongly attached to the problem. Perhaps I don't want to admit that I've made a mistake or was wrong about something. Or I don't want to admit to myself or to my partner my part in the process that has separated us. So, although the steps in this process are pretty straightforward, it's not necessarily an easy path to take.

Consistent effort — persistence in using the process, trusting that there is an answer somewhere, and holding open the possibility are the keys here. When you add these to the kindness and gentleness of the unconditional presence you are holding for yourself, you have a winning combination.

Or if you feel particularly stuck or hopeless, the following phrase can be helpful:

"I'm open to the possibility that this issue is not as it seems, that I am missing something, that there may be another way to see this — the whole truth of this issue may not yet be evident."

Sit quietly with these words and be open to new information. See what pops into your awareness. Watch your dreams. Ask to be shown the whole picture, open again, and listen for the still small voice of deeper wisdom to whisper to you.

Another effective tactic in resolving these stubborn, painful situations is to make a commitment to remember the possibility that you're holding, as you go through each day, in your contact with this person or with the issues that bring up the pain or discomfort within yourself.

Make a commitment to remember it differently.

Make a commitment to be open to the possibility, to expand your perceptual lens around this particular issue, so that if there is another truth to be seen, it will show itself.

And sometimes when we are feeling stuck, we have to look in the mirror. Is a part of you fighting this process because you don't want to admit your role in it? Can you gently hold that part of you and look it in the eyes and admit to yourself that you do have a role in this situation, and without blame or criticism, simply acknowledge it and move on to creating a solution, a new way of seeing yourself and the other person in this situation.

Sometimes as your perceptual lens expands, you are suddenly able to hear people around you telling you things that can help you see your issue in a new way — things that you weren't open to hearing before. And then events spontaneously happen around you that show you things, that help you to see things with new eyes.

When we're present, with our eyes wide open, we learn from everything that happens in our lives, rather than just repeating the same events over and over again. None of us want our most painful events to be repeated over and over. We often just don't see any other way. So, make a commitment to be open to the possibility that you could see things in a new way.

Take a moment now and check in again with the part of you being cradled by your internal healing hands or presence. How does it feel now? As you've considered new possibilities and expanded your perceptual lens, how has that impacted this place? Has it started to shift and expand a little, or a lot? Are you feeling the edges of some new ways to see your situation? Good. Wherever you are with this is fine.

And sometimes the most important step in resolving a tangled, seemingly intractable relationship problem is to make a commitment to set aside time to do this Exploration on a regular basis so that you have a vehicle to move your issue toward resolution, step by step, while holding yourself in a loving, powerful way. So, take a moment to commit to whatever you need to do, no matter how small, if this issue needs more conscious air time from you.

And let this part of you know that, although you are going to take your conscious awareness elsewhere as we finish up, you remain committed to this healing process as long as it takes, whether it takes a few minutes or a few months or a few years.

And now, bring your awareness back to your feet and feel the earth beneath you, soaking up what you need in order to end this process full, with that flow moving through you, feeling ready to bring your awareness back from the internal to the external, feeling full and juicy.

[Pause]

When you are ready, open your eyes and drink in your surroundings. Feel your backbone against your chair. Feel the steadiness of your body. Notice how you feel now compared to when you began.

And enjoy!

To download the free audio tracks for this book or order a CD
for a small fee plus shipping, visit

www.healingfromthecore.com,
click on the Full Body Presence Download link,
and enter the password *presence*

or write to us at

Healing from the Core
P.O. Box 2534
Reston, VA 20195-2534

Resources

We now actually live in a world where the imaginings written in chapter 10 are possible. The available resources and conscious awareness about all of these issues are now growing so quickly that I have added resource pages to my website. This allows these lists to be continually updated. Please visit:

www.healingfromthecore.com or
www.fullbodypresence.com

I encourage you to also sign up for our e-newsletter to learn about new and exciting resources as they become available. Or come attend a Full Body Presence class and experience this work in a safe, supportive group.

It is up to us to choose to go for it, and enjoy!

To write me about your experiences with this book, visit the websites above or contact:

Healing from the Core Media
P.O. Box 2534
Reston, VA 20195-2534

Index

About the Author

Amelia Mitchell

Suzanne Scurlock-Durana, CMT, CST-D, has taught about conscious awareness and its relationship to the healing process for more than twenty-five years. She is passionate about teaching people practical skills that allow them to feel the joy of being present in each moment of their lives, without burning out.

She is a certified instructor of CranioSacral therapy and Somato-Emotional Release with the Upledger Institute. Based on decades of teaching healthcare practitioners how to hold a healing space for themselves and others, Suzanne developed the Healing from the Core curriculum and complementary audio series. She teaches both curriculums internationally. She also provides ongoing staff development training at the Esalen Institute and collaborates regularly with Emilie Conrad, integrating Continuum movement with healing presence.

Known for her honest, grounded, nurturing manner, Suzanne assists others in going to the heart of their healing process. She is adept at weaving together mind, body, and spirit to create a unique environment where profound healing can occur. To accomplish this, she draws on her wealth of experience as a professional, a teacher and a therapist, a wife and a mother, and generously shares from all areas of her life.

A sought-after speaker in her field, Suzanne inspires healthcare providers all over the world to stay energized using her life-changing tools for stress management and Full Body Presence. She also has authored numerous articles, and thousands visit her popular blog, *Presence Matters: Reflections on Body, Mind and Spirit* at http://massage mag.com/massage-blog/presence-matters. She has a private practice in Reston, Virginia, where her clients also benefit from the techniques she teaches. Many of the skills she is known for are in this book.

You can learn more at
www.healingfromthecore.com